THE NEW CAMBRIDGE

GENERAL EDITOR: Brian Gibbons
ASSOCIATE EDITOR: A. R. Braunmuller

From the publication of the first volumes in 1984 the General Editor of the New Cambridge Shakespeare was Philip Brockbank and the Associate General Editors were Brian Gibbons and Robin Hood. From 1990 to 1994 the General Editor was Brian Gibbons and the Associate Editors were A. R. Braunmuller and Robin Hood.

THE FIRST QUARTO OF KING HENRY V

The quarto text of *Henry V* is of unique importance. It has the authority of being transcribed by actors in Shakespeare's own company as a record of their original staging of the play at the Globe in 1599. In this new edition Andrew Gurr argues that the *Henry V* quarto is probably the best surviving example of a Shakespeare playscript as it was actually performed. The speed with which it came to press only a year after its first staging marks its status as an official version of the play first seen by Elizabethan audiences. As a practical staging text it therefore does much to shed new light on what happened to scripts that the Shakespeare company bought from their resident playwright.

The *Henry V* quarto is radically different from the 1623 First Folio version used in all other editions of the play. It is only half as long, eliminating entire scenes, transposing others, shortening long speeches and streamlining the text into something that could easily be put on as a two-hour performance. It has been identified as one of the so-called 'bad' quartos, made up from the memory of actors, but, according to modern theories, this gives it considerable distinction as a record of how the play was staged.

This is the only modernised edition of the *Henry V* quarto in print. Andrew Gurr provides the most extensive commentary to date on the significance and history of the text, and his textual notes examine each variant from the Folio text in detail. The edition is designed to complement the New Cambridge Shakespeare edition of the Folio text (1992), also edited by Professor Gurr.

THE NEW CAMBRIDGE SHAKESPEARE

THE FIRST QUARTO OF
KING HENRY V

Edited by

ANDREW GURR

Professor of Renaissance Studies
University of Reading

CAMBRIDGE
UNIVERSITY PRESS

CAMBRIDGE UNIVERSITY PRESS
Cambridge, New York, Melbourne, Madrid, Cape Town, Singapore, São Paulo

Cambridge University Press
The Edinburgh Building, Cambridge CB2 2RU, UK

Published in the United States of America by Cambridge University Press, New York

www.cambridge.org
Information on this title: www.cambridge.org/9780521623360

First published 2000
This digitally printed first paperback version 2006

A catalogue record for this publication is available from the British Library

Library of Congress Cataloguing in Publication data

Shakespeare, William, 1564–1616.
[Henry V]
The first quarto of King Henry V / edited by Andrew Gurr.
    p.   cm. – (The New Cambridge Shakespeare)
ISBN 0 521 62336 7 (hardback)
1. Henry V, King of England, 1387–1422 – Drama.   2. Great Britain – History – Henry V,
1413–1422 – Drama.   I. Title.   II. Gurr, Andrew.
PR2750.B12   G87   2000
822.3′3 21 – dc21-99-043666

ISBN-13 978-0-521-62336-0 hardback
ISBN-10 0-521-62336-7 hardback

ISBN-13 978-0-521-03263-6 paperback
ISBN-10 0-521-03263-6 paperback

THE NEW CAMBRIDGE SHAKESPEARE
THE EARLY QUARTOS

There is no avoiding edited Shakespeare, the question is only what kind of editing. A Shakespeare play first assumed material form as the author's bundle of manuscript sheets. The company of players required a manuscript fair copy of the play (apart from the individual actors' parts). Into the fair copy were entered playhouse changes, and the bookholder used it during each performance. However, none of Shakespeare's plays survives in contemporary manuscript form. There is one passage in the manuscript of *Sir Thomas More* by Hand D which has been ascribed to Shakespeare himself, but this attribution remains in serious dispute. In short, there is no direct access to Shakespeare's play-manuscripts – there is only print, and this implies editing, since the first printed versions of Shakespeare were mediated by compositors and proofreaders at least, and sometimes also by revisers, bookholders, editors, censors, and scribes. The first printers used either the author's or a playhouse manuscript or some combination of the two, although for several plays they used a scribal transcript by Ralph Crane, who is known to have habitually effaced and altered his copy.

There are certain quartos which are abbreviated, apparently because they are reported texts or derive from playhouse adaptation. These early quartos are not chosen as copy-texts for modern critical editions and are not readily available, though indispensable to advanced students of Shakespeare and of textual bibliography. Alongside the standard volumes in the New Cambridge Shakespeare, editions of selected quarto texts are to be published in critical, modern-spelling form, including early quartos of *King Lear*, *Hamlet*, *Richard III*, and *Othello*.

While the advanced textual scholar must work either with the rare, actual copies of the earliest printed editions, or with photo-facsimiles of them, there is more general interest in these texts and hence a need to present them in a form that makes them more generally accessible, a form that provides the most up-to-date and expert scholarship and engages with the key issues of how these texts differ from other quarto versions and from the First Folio, and to what effect. These are the precise aims of New Cambridge Shakespeare quartos.

Each volume presents, with the text and collation, an introductory essay about the quarto text, its printing, and the nature of its differences from the other early printed versions. There is discussion of scholarly hypotheses about its nature and provenance, including its theatrical provenance, where that issue is appropriate. The accompanying notes address textual, theatrical, and staging questions, following the spacious and handsome format of the New Cambridge Shakespeare.

BRIAN GIBBONS
General Editor

CONTENTS

ILLUSTRATIONS

PREFACE

This edition of the first text of Shakespeare's *Henry V* to appear in print is meant to be complementary to the New Cambridge Shakespeare edition of the Folio text (1992). It follows the practice of the New Cambridge series by modernising the spelling, punctuation and setting-out of the text on the page, and collating the significant variants between the first printed texts. Its commentary notes do not attempt to duplicate those of the NCS edition, and its introductory materials give the stage history and critical views only as they relate specifically to the first quarto text of 1600. The Introduction to this edition leaves the long history of the staging of the Folio text of the play to the edition of the Folio text. Instead it analyses the nature of the copy from which the quarto text was printed, and sets out the case for it being a version closely based on the Shakespeare company's own performance script of the play, a text made for or from its first performances in 1599.

The implications of this view of the two substantive texts of *Henry V* are, to put it mildly, extensive. They indicate that the Folio text, with its famous Choruses and speeches such as Henry's exhortation to his troops before Harfleur, was unlikely to have been heard at the Globe at any time before 1623, and probably not until the play was revived with the aid of the Folio-based editions of the eighteenth century. They suggest that Shakespeare and his company were in the habit of trimming and redrafting his scripts for use on the stage quite drastically. They shortened long speeches and cut redundant characters in order to streamline the text into something that could easily be put on as a two-hour performance. Lacking the respect of later generations for Shakespeare's every word, they used the manuscript which later became the Folio text as the raw material for their own creation, a shorter, brisker, simpler play.

If this view is correct, the quarto text of *Henry V* offers the best evidence we have of what routinely happened to the scripts that the Shakespeare company bought from their resident playwright. No other Shakespeare quarto has the same level of authority: that of a text set from an authorised playhouse manuscript. It is an intelligent and coherent version of the play we have known for centuries as Shakespeare's original idea. It was clearly made for performance on the stages that Shakespeare wrote for. As such, it repays minutely detailed and scrupulous study. The quarto text of *Henry V* has not had much attention from editors until recently. Thought of as no more than a cheap paste copy of the Shakespearean diamond, it was seen as of marginal interest, on the page and in the theatre. Fresh concern for the history of Shakespeare in performance and how his scripts were realised on their original stages makes the quarto the prime case in point to test the view that the plays were radically altered between their first drafting and their first appearance on stage.

Many editors, bibliographers and critics have given attention, marginal though it has been, to the quarto text. This edition sits on their massive shoulders. The more obvious debts are noted in the Introduction and Commentary, and their footnotes. I also owe a substantial and enduring debt to the librarians at the Folger Shakespeare Library and, as always, to my colleagues at the University of Reading. What may be less evident is the long-running and unrepayable debt to Sarah Stanton of Cambridge University Press, and to the General Editors of the NCS and Quarto series, above all Brian Gibbons. Sarah and Brian have been the most consistently reliable supporters and the invaluable safety net for all these editorial acrobatics. And underpinning everything there has always been Libby.

A. G.

Reading

ABBREVIATIONS AND CONVENTIONS

The edition of the Folio text of *Henry V* cited in this edition is that in the New Cambridge Shakespeare (NCS), of 1992. Other editions and critical works are cited under the editor's or author's name (Theobald, Taylor). Shakespeare plays are cited in this edition in the abbreviated style of the series, modified slightly from the *Harvard Concordance to Shakespeare*. Quotations from other plays of Shakespeare are taken from the *Norton Shakespeare*, under the general editorship of Stephen Greenblatt. Norton generally uses the Oxford text of 1986.

Shakespeare's plays

Ado	*Much Ado About Nothing*
Ant.	*Antony and Cleopatra*
AWW	*All's Well That Ends Well*
AYLI	*As You Like It*
Cor.	*Coriolanus*
Cym.	*Cymbeline*
Err.	*The Comedy of Errors*
Ham.	*Hamlet*
1H4	*The First Part of King Henry the Fourth*
2H4	*The Second Part of King Henry the Fourth*
H5	*King Henry the Fifth*
1H6	*The First Part of King Henry the Sixth*
2H6	*The Second Part of King Henry the Sixth*
3H6	*The Third Part of King Henry the Sixth*
H8	*King Henry the Eighth*
JC	*Julius Caesar*
John	*King John*
LLL	*Love's Labours Lost*
Lear	*King Lear*
Mac.	*Macbeth*
MM	*Measure for Measure*
MND	*A Midsummer Night's Dream*
MV	*The Merchant of Venice*
Oth.	*Othello*
Per.	*Pericles*
R2	*King Richard the Second*
R3	*King Richard the Third*
Rom.	*Romeo and Juliet*
Shr.	*The Taming of the Shrew*
STM	*Sir Thomas More*
Temp.	*The Tempest*
TGV	*The Two Gentlemen of Verona*
Tim.	*Timon of Athens*
Tit.	*Titus Andronicus*

TN	*Twelfth Night*
TNK	*The Two Noble Kinsmen*
Tro.	*Troilus and Cressida*
Wiv.	*The Merry Wives of Windsor*
WT	*The Winter's Tale*

Other works cited and general references

Abbott	E. A. Abbott, *A Shakespearian Grammar*, 1894
Capell	*Shakespeare's Comedies, Histories and Tragedies*, ed. Edmund Capell, 10 vols., London, 1767–8, VI
conj.	conjecture
Duthie	G. I. Duthie, 'The Quarto of Shakespeare's *Henry V*', *Papers, Mainly Shakespearian*, Edinburgh: Oliver and Boyd, 1964, pp. 106–30
F	Mr William Shakespeares Comedies, Histories, and Tragedies, 1623 (First Folio)
Jackson	MacDonald P. Jackson '*Henry V*, III, vi, 181: An Emendation', *NQ* n.s. 13 (1996), 133–4
Jonson	*Benjamin Jonson*, ed. C. H. Herford and P. and E. Simpson, 11 vols., Oxford, 1925–52
Malone	*The Plays and Poems of William Shakespeare*, ed. Edmund Malone, 10 vols., 1790, V
Maxwell	J. C. Maxwell, '*Henry V*, II, ii, 103–4', *NQ* 199 (1954), 195
MLN	*Modern Language Notes*
Moore Smith	*Henry V*, ed. G. C. Moore Smith (Warwick, 1893)
NQ	*Notes and Queries*
OED	*The Oxford English Dictionary*
Oxford	*William Shakespeare. The Complete Works*, ed. Stanley Wells and Gary Taylor, Oxford, 1986 (one volume)
Pope	*The Works of Shakespear*, ed. Alexander Pope, 6 vols., 1725, III
Q (Q1)	THE CRONICLE History of Henry the fift, With his battell fought at *Agin Court* in France. Togither with *Auntient Pistoll*. 1600 (first quarto)
Q2	THE CHRONICLE History of Henry the fift, With his battell fought at *Agin Court* in France. *As it hath bene sundry times playd by the Right honorable the Lord Chamberlaine his seruants*. 1602 (second quarto)
Q3	The Chronicle History of Henry the fift, With his battell fought at *Agin Court* in France. *Togither with* Ancient *Pistoll*. 1619 (third quarto)
Rowe	*The Works of Mr. William Shakespear*, ed. Nicholas Rowe, 6 vols., 1709, III
SD	stage direction
SH	speech heading
SQ	*Shakespeare Quarterly*
Steevens	*The Plays of William Shakespeare*, ed. Samuel Johnson and George Steevens, 10 vols., 1773, VI
S.Sur	*Shakespeare Survey*
Taylor	*Henry V*, ed. Gary Taylor, 1982 (New Oxford)
Three Studies	Stanley Wells and Gary Taylor, *Modernising Shakespeare's Spelling, with Three Studies in the Text of 'Henry V'*, Oxford: Clarendon Press, 1979
Theobald	*The Works of Shakespeare*, ed. Lewis Theobald, 7 vols., 1733. IV
TLN	through-line number (used for Folio)

Walter   *Henry V*, ed. J. H. Walter, 1954 (New Arden)
Williams   Gordon Williams, *A Dictionary of Sexual Language and Imagery in Shake-spearean and Stuart Literature*. 3 vols., London, 1994
Wilson   *Henry V*, ed. J. Dover Wilson, 1947 (New Shakespeare)

INTRODUCTION

The significance of the quarto text of *Henry V*

The character of the text of *Henry V* printed in the First Folio of 1623 (F) is not seriously in doubt. As the NCS edition and others argue, it was set from an authorial manuscript that had not been through the developmental process of emendation for performance. The version printed in 1600 (Q), however, tells a different story. It contains several features that show radical corrections made to the F text either in the course of preparing the play for performance or during its first run on stage. It cuts the total number of lines by a half, eliminating entire scenes and transposing others, and shortens or cuts all the longer speeches. The speed with which it came to the press only a year after its first staging is a mark both of its proximity to the text performed by the company that owned it and of its authority as an official version. Between 1598 and 1600 ten plays owned by Shakespeare's company came into print, seven of them Shakespeare's own. With the sole exception of the *Henry V* quarto, and Jonson's *Every Man Out of his Humour*, which Jonson gave to the press himself, all of them were at least three years old. In the speed of its delivery to the press, Q *Henry V* is unique even among the so-called 'bad' quartos. What its text can tell us about its origins and its intended function is uniquely valuable for an understanding of what Shakespeare's company did to adapt the play-manuscripts he sold to them for staging.

The nature of playhouse manuscripts

The written word is almost the only form of record that can tell us in detail what happened in the early modern period of English history. The limitations of such records when they are used to identify any of the more nuanced forms of a culture, such as the original performances of Shakespeare's plays, are self-evident. It is a truism that the written word as a means of recording any spoken and visual script leaves a great deal to be desired. Radio and film nowadays can show nuances and inflexions of speech and gesture that writing can only record by pages of painstaking description. It is likely that the performed text, the only kind of publication that Shakespeare sought for his plays, differed widely from the written versions of the plays that have survived. This makes it necessary to look with caution at the surviving printed texts. In 1986 the Oxford edition of the plays announced that its target was not the hunt for texts as they first left the author's hand, unsullied by alterations of the players and their book-keepers (which had been the object of the 'New Bibliographers' of the early part of this century). Instead Oxford's ideal was conceptually the play as performed in its first appearances by the original company of which Shakespeare was a principal shareholder, and in which he himself regularly acted between 1594 and 1613.[1] When we recognise what a high-speed process it was to produce the plays for original performance, how irregular those original performances were, how liable to change the conditions of playing, and how flexible the text had to be as it was taken from page to stage, we can see that there is little hope of retrieving from the written text much of the original performance, and that a concept of a fixed 'performance text' is a misconception.

Still, the quarto text of *Henry V* is probably closer to the version of the play that Shakespeare's company first put on the stage in 1599 than any form of the play that modern audiences have seen. That it is such an obscure version of Shakespeare's play is a comment on the priority we have given to Shakespeare on the page since the First Folio appeared in 1623, and a comment on the difficulty of recording a performance text simply with words. It is also true that readers find less value in performance scripts than in texts prepared for reading. The text for performance which a company compose from their author's manuscript has always been ranked lower than the original composition itself. The fact that Shakespeare himself made no effort to get his play-manuscripts into print, but was only concerned to have them staged, may indicate that he shared the preference of his original audiences. If so, his choice is not the preference of subsequent generations of readers. The quarto text of *Henry V* printed in 1600 is probably the best surviving example of a Shakespeare play-script as it was first performed by the company that bought it – and Shakespeare was a member of that company. So the quarto text deserves attention as the closest we are ever likely to get to the editorial ideal (or will o'the wisp) of the Oxford edition, Shakespeare in performance at the Globe in 1599.

John Webster made a useful distinction between what he called the 'poem', his own composition, and the 'play', the text actually performed by the play's owners, the players.[2] The differences between the 'poem' and the 'play' in performance are complex, and are made particularly difficult to identify because of the inherently static nature of the one and the inescapably fluid character of the other. Peter Blayney's view, shared with several hundreds of theatre directors, is that 'the author's final draft is essentially only the raw material for performance'.[3] Blayney separates the two versions even further from each other than did the New Bibliographers, who kept the author's draft separate from the theatre copy (which they used to call, anachronistically, the 'promptbook'). In the lengthy and fluid collaborative process of getting a play from page to stage, no single moment ever existed when a written script, a uniquely authoritative record of the 'performance text', could be established.

The playing conditions of Shakespeare's time made the growth of differences between the original company's own written playbook and the text the players performed inevitable. The author's script was designed from the outset to be an idealised, maximal text, and every early performance altered it into more realistic or realisable

[1] Oxford, p. xxxv.
[2] *The Works of John Webster*, ed. David Gunby, David Carnegie, and Antony Hammond, Cambridge, 1995, 1.35–9.
[3] *The First Folio of Shakespeare: The Norton Facsimile*, second edition, New York, 1996, p. xxx.

shapes, often at a quite drastic remove from the ideal.[1] The standard practices of the early companies did require them to possess an 'ideal' text of their plays. It was what the players themselves saw as their maximal version of the text, but it was not quite what modern editors seek to retrieve. Modern printed editions of the plays of Shakespeare and his fellow writers present ideal texts unlikely to have been staged in full on any of the original stages. Every early playing company's ideal was a 'maximal' text. It had a highly specific identity, and an absolutely authorising function. It was the players' manuscript that the Master of the Revels had read and 'allowed' for playing, at the end of which his signature was appended. Today we might call it the 'playscript', the unique manuscript held by the players as their authorisation for whatever version they might perform. The Folio version of *Henry V* probably approximates to such a 'maximal' text. The quarto version represents something much closer to the 'minimal' text that was actually performed.

It was inherently unlikely that many of the early playbooks rewritten for performance would survive their use by the playing companies. They were too valuable to the companies to be used for printing. The manuscripts employed to print the plays were usually the less precious copies not needed for company use. Conjectures about the source manuscripts for Shakespeare's own plays, either in the quartos or in the Folio, range from the manuscript or 'foul papers' that the author first delivered to the company, to a version of the company's own 'playbook' (usually miscalled by editors the 'prompt copy'),[2] transcribed from the author's copy and modified for performance. Some, conceivably though implausibly, might have been the authorised performance copy, a 'maximal' text. Others are thought to be defective scripts assembled by a group of players who made up their text by writing out the lines they remembered from the original performances. Within that wide range, varying from the author's own hand telling what he hoped would be enacted to copies made after a run of performances by some of the players out of their memories, either as an alternative record of the performed text or as a more fanciful text for the reader, lie a whole series of likely transcriptions, any or all of which might have modified the original authorial intention.

The maximal text, however, was not the one that the players normally or even ever performed. Jonson, Webster and others took care to see that it was their maximal texts which appeared in print, usually joined to a complaint that the players had not used them. Richard Brome complained of the difference between the curtailed text that was performed and his 'allowed' playscript on the titlepage of his *Antipodes*, printed in 1640. He justified printing his text by claiming that '*You shal find in this Booke more then was presented upon the* Stage, *and left out of the* Presentation, *for superfluous length (as some of the* Players *pretended) I thogt good al should be inserted according to the allowed*

---

[1] A more extended version of this argument is in Gurr, 'Maximal and Minimal Texts: Shakespeare versus the Globe', *S.Sur* 52 (2000), 68–87.
[2] The early companies did use a 'prompter', but his job was not to give the players their lines when they forgot them. The nineteenth-century version of the term that we know is an anachronism in the Elizabethan theatre. See William B. Long, 'Perspective on Provenance: The Context of Varying Speech-heads', in *Shakespeare's Speech-Headings*, ed. George Walton Williams, Newark, NJ, 1997, p. 24.

Original'. Authors' texts and players' texts differed above all in length, much as Q1 *Henry V* differs from its Folio version.

The history of *Henry V*'s quarto text

The thought that the quarto version of *Henry V* was a reasonably good acting text has been around for some time, although no acting company has ever put it into practice. In 1970 Ivor Brown, in *Shakespeare and the Actors*, said that the idea is 'held by some' that the quarto is 'an acting version' of the play used by the Lord Chamberlain's Men, to deliver a shorter version than the Folio.[1] This was a less than scholarly view, reflecting more of Brown's own theatre experience than any close study of the two texts.

The idea that Shakespeare revised his texts, which has hung particularly strongly on the early versions of *2* and *3 Henry VI*, also attached itself in the early days of the New Bibliography to the first quartos of *Henry V*, *Romeo and Juliet*, and *The Merry Wives of Windsor*. In 1919 John Dover Wilson, in association with Alfred Pollard, broached the idea that these quartos were the product of the hard times for Strange's Men in 1593. A lengthy correspondence in the *Times Literary Supplement* ran from January till August, mainly over the very concept that Shakespeare might have revised his own work. Wilson eventually renounced this early concept, and in his New Shakespeare edition of *Henry V* in 1947 he took the traditional line that the Q text was a 'bad' or pirated version.

The history of ideas about the relationship between Q1 and F is complex, though it does show an intermittent evolution towards the idea that Q may have some authority, if not as an authorial text then as a performance text. The Folio, however, is the text that from the 1660s onwards always formed the basis for stage productions. In the late nineteenth and early twentieth centuries *Henry V* was the play most studied in schools, especially for its Choruses and Henry's two great speeches, Harfleur and the band of brothers. Only one of these highlights is in the quarto text. The early players of Shakespeare had not acquired the massive reverence for the master's text and its great setpieces that we have inherited, and that critical judgements have repeatedly confirmed.

Recent changes in views about the *Henry V* quarto started by questioning the general assumption that it was a 'bad' text corrupted by theatrical input and imperfect forms of transmission, one of the species that Heminges and Condell in their preface to the first Folio called 'Stolne and surreptitious copies'. The quartos identified as the targets for this dismissive assumption were thought to have contaminated the purity of Shakespeare's poetry with theatrical mud. Moreover, through almost all of the nineteenth and twentieth centuries it was assumed that Q was a 'memorial' reconstruction, made by a few actors from their memory of what they had performed, so even as a theatre script it had to be second-hand. This led to the view that it had been made up for use by a small company touring the provinces, so that again even as a performed text it was seen as second-quality theatre. The evidence of the text itself upholds none of these views.

---

[1] Ivor Brown, *Shakespeare and the Actors*, London: Bodley Head, 1970, p. 62.

THE

CRONICLE

Hiſtory of Henry the fift,

With his battell fought at *Agin Court* in
France. Togither with *Auntient*
Piſtoll.

As it hath bene ſundry times playd by the Right honorable
the Lord Chamberlaine his ſeruants.

LONDON

Printed by *Thomas Creede*, for Tho. Millington, and Iohn Busby. And are to be
ſold at his houſe in Carter Lane, next
the Powle head. 1600.

The title page of the first quarto, 1600

The quarto printings

The printing of the different versions of *Henry V* began in 1600, within a year of its composition and first staging. It was evidently a popular text, as its publishing history shows. The title of the quarto printed in 1600 advertised that its attractions included 'Auntient Pistoll', possibly making a tacit acknowledgement that it did not contain Sir John Falstaff, as promised by the epilogue that appeared with the first quarto of *2 Henry IV*, also printed in 1600. The first quarto of *2 Henry IV* was entered in the Stationers' Register on 23 August, a week after a mysterious 'staying' order about a group of four Shakespeare plays. But by then the first quarto of *Henry V* had appeared or was about to appear.

The much-discussed 'staying entry' in the Stationers' Register of 4 August 1600, held back the registration for printing of four Chamberlain's Men's plays, *As You Like It*, *Henry V*, *Every Man in his Humour* and *Much Ado about Nothing*. Its circumstances have been dealt with in the NCS edition (pp. 216–20), where it is concluded that it was more likely to be a reference to *2 Henry IV* than *Henry V*. The first time the Stationers' Register took note of the text for the quarto *Henry V* was ten days later, on 14 August, when Thomas Pavier registered it as one of several titles he had acquired the right to issue. The name registered is the same as that on the first quarto's titlepage. It recorded Pavier's acquisition of the name so that he could get Thomas Creede, who had already issued the first quarto on the authority of his 1594 entry in the Register for *The Famous Victories of Henry V*, to print a second quarto, which he did in 1602. The fact that Pavier bought the copy and paid to register his right to print it indicates that the first quarto was already on sale and doing well.

The quarto of *Henry V* was not entered for printing in the Stationers' Register in 1600, because Thomas Creede had already entered his copy for *The Famous Victories* back in 1594. He printed that text in 1598, and his successor issued it again in 1617. He issued his Chamberlain's Men's quarto, Q1, some time before August 1600, on behalf of Thomas Millington and John Busby, who marketed it. They were all respectable men in their occupations. Creede had printed *The Contention*, a version of *2 Henry VI*, for Millington in 1594, and other play-texts since then, including the second quarto of *Richard III* for Andrew Wise in 1598 and in 1599 the 'corrected' second quarto of *Romeo and Juliet*. Millington also re-issued in 1600 the second quarto of *The True Tragedy*, the shorter version of *3 Henry VI*. Creede went on to print the second quarto of *Henry V* for the new owner, Thomas Pavier, in 1602. Such an early reprint was a good reflection of its popularity among buyers, matching *Romeo and Juliet*, *Richard II*, *Richard III* and *1 Henry IV* and its Falstaff through those years. In 1619 Pavier issued a third quarto misleadingly dated 1608, the last before the very different Folio version came out in 1623.[1]

---

[1] Its two quartos of 1600 and 1602, and the reprint of 1619, rank it next to *Romeo and Juliet*, the two *Richards*, *1 Henry IV*, and *Titus Andronicus* as the most in demand of Shakespeare's early plays. See Mark Bland, 'The London Book-Trade in 1600', in *A Companion to Shakespeare*, ed. D. S. Kastan, Oxford: Blackwell, 1999, pp. 450–63, p. 461. The marginal significance of playbooks in general as material for the press is emphasised by Peter W. M. Blayney, 'The Publication of Playbooks', in *A New History of the Early English Drama*, ed. John D. Cox and David Scott Kastan, New York: Columbia University Press, 1997, pp. 383–422.

Five copies of Q1 and one fragment have survived. The complete copies are at the British Library, the Bodleian, Wren, Huntington, and Yale Libraries, and the Folger Shakespeare Library has the first seven leaves of another copy (A1–B3v). Three copies of Q2 survive, at the Wren, Huntington and Folger Libraries, and several of the Pavier Q3, including one each at the Huntington, Folger, New York Public and University of Illinois Libraries. I have examined the British Library and Wren Library copies of Q1, and facsimiles of the Bodleian and Huntington Library copies, together with the Folger fragment of Q1 and its copies of Q2 and Q3. None of the quartos show any corrections made while the work was in press.

The nature of the copy used to set Q1 is the largest of the many questions about the text, but the printing of the quarto itself was relatively straightforward. Only one compositor set the text, and he did so rather casually, or intermittently, setting by formes, with a break of some kind between setting sigs. E and F, and F and G.[1] The copy for the text was evidently far from easy for the compositor. He set every line in his text as verse, capitalising the first letter, and never justifying to the right margin as prose. In doing this he must have followed the lineation of his manuscript copy, where the copyist, receiving dictation, set down each line as he received it. Taking the text down from dictation is evident throughout scene 1, in the frequency of short lines, the number of mishearings, and (compared with the F text) lines divided in half and lines that run on with extra phrases.

The second quarto (Q2) added a few compositorial adjustments to the Q1 text, and introduced several new errors. Q1's 'lide' at 1.197 was corrected to 'like', '*Nims*' at 2.25 became '*Nim*', and Q1's 'the the' at 17.4 was also corrected; Q1's 'so full of' at 1.199 was miscorrected to 'with so full of'. A line of text at 14.13 was italicised as a stage direction; Q1's '*Barbasom*' became '*Earbasom*', conceivably because the copy of Q1 used in setting Q2 had a broken capital B; less sensibly 'Sutler' at 2.67 became 'Butler', a rather comic misunderstanding; and errors of eyeskip and dittography appear at 11.84 and 17.23. A monosyllable was inserted at 19.80, two omitted at 10.8 and 12.88, and 'my rest' became 'the rest' at 2.16. The most purposeful change was at 12.82, where Q1's 'are in the' became 'within are'. Curiously, the phonetic spelling of Llewellyn's 'Ieshu', employed with some deliberateness by the Q3 compositor, also turns up in Q2 at 11.24, replacing Q1's normative 'Iesu'.

The third quarto (Q3), printed in 1619 with the date '1608' on its titlepage, was the ninth of ten so-called 'Pavier quartos', all printed at about the same time by the same bookseller with similarly false early dates. Pavier, as holder of the right to print quite a few of the play-texts, was soon to be involved in the printing of the first Folio. His Compositor 'B' set a large section of the Folio, and B's habits in type-setting that text are well known from what he did when setting from surviving printed copy. It was he who set the whole of *Henry V* Q3.[2]

The copy for Q3 was clearly Q1. Its compositor ignored several instances of Q2's

---

[1] Thomas L. Berger has done a careful analysis of the printing, described in 'The Printing of *Henry V*, Q1', *The Library*, 6th series, 1 (1979), 114–25.

[2] See Peter W. M. Blayney, ' "Compositor B" and the Pavier Quartos: Problems of Identification and their Implications', *The Library* 27 (1972), 179–206.

alterations, and in seven cases followed Q1 rather than Q2 where there was good reason to copy Q2.[1] On occasions the Q3 compositor's habits were intrusive on the copy of Q1 he used, as they were in the Folio. In general, he followed Q1 carefully, picking up only the more obvious corrections, and sometimes adding or deleting monosyllables to improve the metre or the grammar. He copied Q1's practice of setting every line as verse, except for the beginning of the first Eastcheap scene. When starting to set the inner forme of scene 2, at the head of sig. B1v, he set Bardolph's first three-line speech on that page (lines 13–14) as prose, with lower-case initial letters and justifying the line at the right margin. He started to do the same for the next speech by Nim, but changed his mind after the first line and began setting it as verse. On the outer forme, at the beginning of the scene, on B1, he set it all as verse. His only other uses of lower-case letters to start a line were (mistakenly) for the two short speeches of Gower and Llewellyn at 9.12 and 13. Altogether, the Q3 compositor made enough changes to raise a tricky question for editors of the Folio *Henry V*: whether his changes in Q3 might have affected the Folio version.

More important for this edition is whether his alterations to Q1 came from his consultation of a superior text, or whether he was doing his usual job, evidenced in the sections of the Folio he set, of 'improving' the text as he went along. Most of the changes in Q3 are routine: altering verb ellipses ('here's' for 'here is'), using connectives or prefixes to expand a line, often to improve the metre, putting brackets round parenthetical phrases,[2] improving Q1's French (at 19.66), transposing words, altering a royal 'I' to 'we' (an intensification of Q1's pattern), correcting bad grammar such as 'was' for F's 'were' after a plural pronoun at 16.96, and on two occasions adding touches of text.[3] He also made at least twenty small errors of omission, wrong fount, or other slips,[4] even sometimes cutting a word to make his line fit, as at 4.13; and at 5.9 he replaced Q1's 'busied' with 'troubled', for no obvious reason. None of these changes required any special access to a better text. He also tidied up the Crispin/Crispianus names sensibly. But one very precise alteration and a few less tangible ones need special consideration. The prime case is Q3's alteration of Q1's 'scene' at 9.56 to 'sconce'. The latter is a much less common term for a defensive earthwork than the one used by Gower in Q1, which might have resulted from a misreading of the manuscript. But F has the same word as Q3. Did the Q3 compositor have privileged access to the manuscript he was later to use to set F, or was it an inspired guess? That seems unlikely. Interference between Q3 and F has no direct bearing on Q1, but it does call in question whether the F text is entirely independent

[1] 11.24: Iesu (Q2 Ieshu); 11.77 a nasse (Q2 an asse); 13.8 to the field (Q2 to field); 16.53 yet a many (Q2 yet many); 16.66 take no scorne (Q2 not scorne); 19.80 subscribed this (Q2 subscribed to this); 19.93 full course (Q2 full recourse).
[2] Unmarked parenthetical phrases go into brackets at 1.39, 8.3 and 18, and 9.95; the metre is polished at 1.116, 184 and 213; Q1's short lines are often adjusted, and the text trimmed, as at 2.23–4; Dame Quickly is changed from an adverb to a proper name; Nim's name (2.25) is corrected, as it is in Q2; a wrong tense is changed at 16.96; and Q3 corrects obvious misprints like Q1's 'lide' at 1.197, as does Q2.
[3] At 12.45 he added a phrase to Henry's speech, and at 18.24.1 he inserted a stage direction.
[4] For instance at 9.20 'God's' for Q1's 'godes', meaning goddess; 'out' for 'and' at 2.66; 'winde is' for 'windes' 3.8; a line omitted at 3.19; and 'incarnste' at 4.19.

of Q1, or whether Q1's relation to Q3 was continued by Q3 into F, so it needs some consideration here.

In three cases besides the instance of 9.56 Q3 and F agree against Q1. At 4.25 Q3 shortens Q1's 'hell fire' to 'hell', as in F; at 16.59, instead of Q1's 'Cryspin, Cryspin', Q3 has F's 'Crispin, Crispianus'. And at 12.45 Q3 has an intriguing insertion, the phrase 'They were not there'. It is remarkably close to F's 'they were not here', but could be no more than a coincidental augmentation, not unlike the stage direction added to Q3 specifying that Pistol eats Llewellyn's leek at 18.24. The phrase does strengthen the grammar, and might have been added independently. Of the other two cases, the coincidence of setting 'Hell' instead of 'hell fire' is easy to swallow on the same terms. Only 'sconce' for 'scene' and the resolution of the 'Crispin' problem in the same way as F pose real challenges to editors who are determined to keep the F manuscript unsullied by Q3. Even the 'Cryspin' coincidence might be explained as the independent choice of a reasonably studied compositor who was concerned to preserve a good metrical pattern. On balance, the one real coincidence, 'sconce', seems insufficient to make a case for any independent authority in the Q3 reviser. The clearest and most characteristic feature of Q3 at its best is at 15.28, where Q1, copied by Q2, omits 'had', an essential verb. Q1 has 'but I not so much'. Q3's correction, which is also in F, was a simple change to make better sense of the line. For this and other changes such inventiveness is to be applauded. The problems the Q3 compositor creates are only crucial if one is looking for the Shakespearean original rather than the record of what was spoken in the play as it was first staged.

The copy for and printing of Q1

The case made in this edition is that the manuscript behind the quarto text was based ultimately on the authorial manuscript sold to Shakespeare's playing company (the Lord Chamberlain's Servants), in 1599 and later printed as the F text, but was a copy which had been radically revised by the company for performance at the Globe. It was put together for performance in London and elsewhere in late 1599 or early 1600 by several members of the company. It was undoubtedly an authoritative players' text. At least two, possibly more, of the company's players who had speaking parts shared the work. Most of the manuscript was recorded by dictation, chiefly from the rough playscript, helped in places by the players' memories of their parts. On occasions there may also have been some resort to an authorial manuscript, either the one later used to set the Folio text, or one close to it, possibly a 'maximal' copy of the author's papers.

Somewhere close behind the manuscript copied for the press in 1600 and printed as Q1 was a carefully planned adaptation, designed to make a viable two-hour script for acting. It makes all the theatrical adjustments needed for a play running at a higher speed and more concisely than the original text as the Folio version gives it, economising on characters, sharpening their exchanges and shortening the longest speeches. Besides abbreviating the author's text by almost a half, it strengthens the heroic aspects, cuts out the references to the king killing Falstaff, and makes consistent alterations to names and other features. The manuscript that was taken down by dictation for the press from this adapted playhouse copy was designed to be read rather than performed, but it was also designed to represent the play as it had been seen at the Globe in 1599 and early 1600.

The changes made for the staged version had a radical effect on what John Arden once called 'a secret play inside the official play'.[1] The number of spoken lines in the text was shortened by a half, from the Folio text's 3,253 lines (Kathleen Irace's count)[2] to 1,629. Prologue, Epilogue and all the Choruses disappeared, and nearly 50 per cent of Henry's speeches, mostly by cutting sections from the lengthier ones, along with three whole scenes. The image of Henry as hero, so emphasised by the Chorus despite the discrepancies between what he says and the staged events he describes, was consistently strengthened. The scaling ladders, an awkward problem for the staging, and for the interpretation of the assault on Harfleur, were cut, as was Henry's 'Once more unto the breach' exhortation. The number of roles was cut, and the doubling of parts made easier. Most of the non-speaking characters were eliminated, and some of the smaller speaking parts were merged into others. Q1 cuts out altogether the Bishop of Ely, Westmorland, Bedford, Sir Thomas Erpingham, Jamy and Macmorris, Queen Isabel, Grandpre, Brittany, Rambures and the English Herald as speaking parts. The decision to cut the Dauphin from Agincourt, which Shakespeare appears to have reached in the course of writing his F text, was upheld by transferring all of his later speeches to Bourbon. The result was a more economical play that could easily be staged by a cast of fifteen or fewer. Tighter in construction and far less laden with long speeches, it would have run for no more than two hours. It cut some of F's imperfections, such as the army departure from Dover rather than Southampton, and it tidied up a number of other staging difficulties.

The most notable changes were made to Act 3, and the siege of Harfleur. The story of that preliminary battle is not merely truncated but transformed. The initial attack on the breach, with its scaling ladders and Henry's celebrated exhortation, disappears, as does the scene with the four captains. What is left is simply Henry's confrontation with the Governor on the walls, preceded by Llewellyn's skirmish with the Eastcheap cowards. This removes the tacit point of the scaling ladders in the F text, which is that the soldiers who climb them onto the stage balcony must be killed and the attack on the breach fail, since the next scene shows the Governor on the same balcony still holding the town. The failure of Henry's 'breach' speech in conquering the town is a tacit feature of the F text, although the Chorus's persuasiveness has been sufficient to let several centuries of readers miss the point.

Compiled during the play's first year of performance at the Globe, the copy that formed the basis for the quarto text is almost certainly the ideal that was announced for the Oxford Shakespeare but not presented there – that is to say, the play as first staged in Shakespeare's presence, not the older ideal, the text as Shakespeare delivered it to

[1] The discrepant views of the play have also been called the 'rabbit and duck' concept, a *gestalt* reading which admits the observer's predisposition. See James N. Loehlin, *Shakespeare in Performance: 'Henry V'*, Manchester: Manchester University Press, 1996; and Norman Rabkin, 'Rabbits, Ducks, and *Henry V*', *SQ* 28 (1977), 279–96.

[2] Kathleen Irace, 'Reconstruction and Adaptation in Q *Henry V*', *Studies in Bibliography* 44 (1991), 228–53, p. 233. This calculation is based on the number of lines spoken, and excluding all stage directions.

the players. The Oxford ideal is specified as 'a text presenting the play as it appeared when performed by the company of which Shakespeare was a principal shareholder in the theatres that he helped to control and on whose success his livelihood depended'.[1] In so far as any written text can be said to represent a performed text, that is what the quarto, and not the Folio version, most distinctly offers.

From a perspective familiar with the poetic riches of the F text, the losses were of course considerable. Most of them, even though they include the Chorus's praise of Henry, help to emphasise the king's heroism at the cost of the play's 'secret' other. The Chorus's six inflationary and coercive speeches were cut entirely, saving 223 lines. The entire opening scene, where the Archbishop explains his plan to distract Henry from the idea of sequestering a large portion of church lands by the promise of financial support for a war in France, and thus discredits his impartiality in expounding the case about Salic Law, was cut. The siege of Harfleur was reduced to sections of comic by-play and Henry's threats to the Governor, eliminating both Henry's famous speech exhorting his soldiers to enter the city at the breach and the scaling ladders that Shakespeare expected to illustrate the failure of the assault. One scene between the French nobles at Agincourt also vanished, along with much of their French.

The cuts caused several difficulties, notably where they affected the usual pattern where characters who leave at the end of one scene never re-enter to start the next one. There are three such cases in Q, mostly as consequences of the cuts and scene-switching. At the end of scene 11 Gloucester leaves with the king, and immediately returns to start scene 12 with Clarence, Exeter and Salisbury. Pistol exits with his French prisoner and the Boy at the end of scene 14, and the stage direction beginning scene 15 specifies that he immediately re-enters with the king and his nobles. He is not present for this scene, where the king orders the cutting of the prisoners' throats, in the F version. Llewellyn and Gower exit with the king at the end of scene 17, and both re-enter to start scene 18. The first of these comes from a confusion of stage directions in Q, discussed below; the second is in part a consequence of switching two scenes in F, 4.4 and 4.6; the third comes from the cut of the Chorus for Act 5 between the two scenes in F.

These changes in Q from the F text have substantial implications for the character of the Q text. It was never a habit with Shakespeare or his contemporary writers to allow exiting players to make immediate re-entries.[2] So either the Q text was not prepared for the stage, or the company working with the version of the play that generated the Q text were in the habit of allowing immediate re-entries. The copyists who made up the manuscript for the press might well have thought of it as a script just for reading, as the NCS edition conjectured. That may explain a few other features noted below, which seem to make it rather a reading text than a theatre playscript.

It was, however, entirely possible to stage these exits and re-entrances at the Globe. There were two usual forms of entry: first, using both of the doors flanking the *frons*

[1] Oxford, p. xxxv.
[2] See Gary Taylor, 'The Structure of Performance: Act Intervals in the London Theatres, 1576–1642', in *Shakespeare Reshaped, 1606–1623*, ed. Gary Taylor and John Jowett, Oxford, 1993.

scenae, when one character enters by one door and meets another coming through the other door, as in *A Midsummer Night's Dream* 2.1, where Oberon greets his queen with 'Ill met by moonlight, proud Titania', or Q *Henry V* 12.21, where Gower hails Llewellyn and is told to speak more quietly; second, when two characters entered through the same door in mid-speech, as in 3.1 of Q *Henry V*, where the English lords enter discussing the conspiracy. For a character to exit and then quickly cross backstage and re-enter was possible when the new entry was by the flanking door not used for the exit, and a procession or group of characters was starting the new scene. That was possible for all of Q's three instances, each of which required several characters to make their entrance before the one who had just left by the other door had to join them. The one radical change was Pistol's re-entry in scene 15. Its implications for the reshaping of the Q text are substantial.

It would not have been difficult for Pistol to pass backstage when he exited by one door at the end of scene 14 to re-enter at the end of Henry's train of nobles for scene 15. The need for him to do so is marked by the addition of his catchphrase 'Couple gorge' as the scene's exit line. Why he should be given that, except as an inflation of his comic role, needs a comment. The Q revisers did something to moderate all the possibly hostile comments on Henry, notably cutting the dialogue about Falstaff's death being caused by the king banishing him. Here it seems that Pistol's words were added in order to tone down the horror of Henry's order to kill the prisoners, the only item of the 'secret' play from F that the revisers retained. The fact that the third re-entry, Gower and Llewellyn after Agincourt, removed the F text's anomaly whereby the Chorus takes the scene back to England and to France again before Llewellyn can get his revenge on Pistol, may have been less deliberate.

The so-called 'reporters' of Q1

Previous analyses of Q1, most notably by G. I. Duthie,[1] worked on the assumption that the copy was provided by a pair of 'reporters', who pirated the copy for the Q text by writing down what they remembered of the text from their own performances. Even Kathleen Irace's computer analysis was affected by this assumption.[2] Such analyses start from the view that the Q lines closest to those of the F text are those of Exeter and Gower, who must therefore have been the pirates responsible for the transcription. Pistol is sometimes considered a helper too, possibly doubling as the Archbishop of Canterbury, whose lines in the opening scene are also close to those in F. Sadly, the assumption that Q was stolen by an act of piracy prevented Duthie, Irace and the others from taking note of the fact that Henry's lines are also, apart from the cuts in his longer speeches, just as closely parallel to those in the F version as those of Exeter and Gower. The player of Henry, assuming he was the company's leader, Richard Burbage, could not conceivably have been a pirate of his own text. Perhaps one might argue that his lines, like those of Pistol, were more memorable to the piratical players

---

[1] Duthie, pp. 106–30.
[2] Kathleen Irace, *Reforming the 'Bad' Quartos: Performance and Provenance of Six Shakespearean First Editions*, Newark, NJ: University of Delaware Press, 1994.

than those of the others. The accuracy of his speeches in Q, however, makes it far more likely that the whole text was printed from a transcription which was fully authorised, and that the players of Exeter and Gower were the two delegated by the company to make the transcription for the press. It was logical to ask two players to do the work, since that allowed one to read the text and the other to write it down. It is worth noting that in 1599 and 1600, when a substantial number of the most popular Chamberlain's Men's plays got into print, the Burbages and several of the players had a special reason for needing extra income, to pay for their new playhouse.

As a consequence of this interpretation of the text, the old terminology has to be changed. Like the idea of a 'bad' quarto, and its association of thieving and the notorious 'stolne and surreptitious copies' put down by Heminges and Condell in the first Folio, the 'reporters' here become 'transcribers' or 'revisers'. The markedly high quality of the copying not just through the Exeter and Gower passages but in those of Pistol and Henry himself strongly hints at the likelihood that a written text was available, and was consulted for the major verse speeches. The Q text is at its worst in the prose scenes, where large cuts were made and the sequence of jokes was re-ordered, and in the verse scenes on each side of major cuts. The prose scenes, however, are still entirely coherent, and the cuts and alterations chiefly indicate only a desire to abbreviate them.

The surviving text in Q1 is some way from being a perfect representation of what was actually said and done on stage in 1599. It has confusions that come from the revision of the original copy to make an acting version as well as mistakes made in the process of transcription, not only by the copyists but by the Q compositor. Each error might come from any one of the steps in the process. We must start with the last level, slips in the printing made by the Q compositor.

Compositor errors in Q1

The sole Q1 compositor did not have an easy task. Presumably because of the nature of his manuscript copy, he set the play entirely as verse, capitalising first lines and leaving plenty of blank space at the end of most lines. He was relatively lavish with the space he had, indenting speech headings, and using nearly empty lines when lines turned out to be too long and needed a turn-under on an extra line. At the end, where he could have saved two leaves or half a gathering by compressing the last ten lines of his text, he spread it to occupy an extra half-page, leaving two and a half pages of blank paper. He misassigned G2 as G3, which may reflect a problem with the space he thought would be available to complete the setting of the last formes.[1] Setting by formes, which requires casting off copy by predicting how much space it would need, depends on reliable line-counts, and this was clearly not an easy task. He may have chosen to set his copy in generously spaced verse because the manuscript did not make

---

[1] The last gathering is numbered G1 and G3, with no G2, and the third leaf (the real G3) is blank. In the other gatherings only the fourth leaf is left blank. This might suggest either that the compositor tried to conceal his extravagance in using the extra leaves, or that he used a thoroughly eccentric configuration for the last pair of formes.

it easy to calculate the necessary allocation of pages. The stage directions vary considerably in the amount of leading that separates them from the spoken text, another indication of the difficulty he had calculating the space the copy needed. Sig. F outer, for instance, has no leading before or after its stage directions, whereas F inner was given a space above and sometimes below. At the same time, his use of spaces in his compositor's stick was characteristically tight. He never used a space after a comma or sometimes a colon, although terminal colons were usually given a space before the colon.

The titlepage occupies A1, the outer forme, A(o). The verso, A1v, is blank. At the end of the first page of the text proper, A2, the compositor added a catchword, '*Bish.*', for the next speech heading, but omitted the speech heading itself on A2v. By the second gathering he was in better control, using '*Nim.*' for the catchword on B2, the inner forme, but '*Nim.* I' on B1, the outer, where the identical catchword could have been confusing. There are, none the less, four errors with catchwords in all, out of the fifty in the complete text, mostly with speech headings. At 12.55 '*King.* Why' is set as the catchword for E2 but the speech heading was omitted from the head of the next page.

Another catchword error says something about the copy he set from. On page D4v of Q he mistakenly used '*Lord*' instead of his regular '*Sol.*' for the two speech headings at 68, and 72 of Scene 11 and in the catchword for the speech heading at 75. Berger[1] calculates the reason for this as the sequence of composing, D (o) followed by D (i), and then E (o). This would have meant that, if the soldiers were simply identified by numbers in the Q manuscript, the compositor, having cast off his copy for sig. E with its '*foure French Lords*', would have assumed on his first encounter with the scene on setting D (o) that the numbers referred to the lords, and so set them on D4v as '3 *Lord.*' and '2. *L*', with the catchword '2.*Lord*'. Then, when setting D (i) he found that D4 specified three soldiers, he changed the speech headings, continuing with the correct designations into sig. E, and correcting the text picked up in D4v's catchword from '2.*Lord*' to '2.*Sol.*'

Other errors in the setting were more routine slips, some of which may also reflect the compositor's difficulty with the copy. At 1.195 'in throne' is a compositor eyeskip, and for the same reason at 15.28 'had' is omitted, damaging both sense and metre. At 1.197 'lide' for 'like' is probably a wrong fount, the kind of error that recurs elsewhere. Other likely wrong-fount errors appear at 3.70 ('haah' for 'hath'), 7.11 ('tude', for 'coude': most likely a wrong-fount error, since the two previous citations have 'c'), and 18.11 (an italic 'I' in Pistol's first speech). Q's 'mistresse quickly' on B1 (2.8) may be a compositor's misreading of the copy's uncapitalised name as an adverb, although the stage direction at B1v on the other forme has '*Hostes Quickly his wife*'. Elsewhere she is '*Nell*' or in the speech headings '*Host.*' The lower-case 'quandom quickly' at B2 on the other forme (2.49) may repeat this confusion. The spelling 'combind' for 'combine' at 2.66 may be a compositor's d/e misreading of the copy, and 'occrue' four lines below may be an a/o misreading. At 8.2 the Constable's 'spranes' in Q is possibly a compositor misreading as two minim strokes for the one in F's 'spraies'.

[1] Berger, 'The Printing of *Henry V*, Q1', p. 120.

There is of course no ready way to determine whether a slip can be identified as the result of error by either compositor, or copy, or its scribe. The difficulty shows up most clearly at 3.57's 'quit in vs', for F's 'quick in us'. It may be equally a compositor's misreading, or a wrong fount, or it might possibly be a viable alternative, although it is less conventional than F. It is equally conceivable that the manuscript copyist might have misheard his fellow's dictation. It is impossible to assign many of these manifest errors to any one cause with complete confidence. The omission of so many '*Exit*' directions, for instance, might equally be casualness on the part of the revisers, for all their theatre experience, or be the result of the compositor's struggle with an illegible manuscript. Overconfidence in ascribing errors to one cause or another leads into a circular argument: this looks like a mishearing, therefore the text must all have been copied from memory; this looks like a wrong fount, therefore the compositor must be responsible for all the errors. Local instances of error indicate local conditions of transcription. Generalisations about the nature of the transcription process need to take all the possible causes of error into account. Circular arguments are inescapable: the most frequent local causes of error have to be used to set up general conclusions about the transmission process as a whole, and therefore give the majority of local verdicts better credibility.

The problems with the Q text in the speech headings are most likely compositorial. Pistol gets a speech heading on successive lines at 11.10. Gower is variously spelled *Gour* on D3, D4 and E4v, and *Gower* on C2v, F1, F3v and F4. More substantially, at 17.45 Q turns directly to the naming of the French prisoners, as if Exeter had been holding the list while the game with the soldier went on. It fails to mark any entry for the herald who delivers the paper in F. In F Henry takes the list of the French dead and then asks Exeter to name the prisoners of the nobility. He then reads the list of dead, starting at what Q makes into Exeter's fifth line. Possibly a speech heading for the king was omitted in Q at line 49, or more likely at line 59. In either case Exeter's line at the end makes it clear that the necessary speech heading is omitted in Q.

Mishearings from dictation

The Quarto text has in abundance the anticipations and recollections from omitted parts of the Folio text which show that the transcribers were familiar with a manuscript that was pretty close to F. Earlier interpretations of the identity of Q have been dominated by the assumption that the copy was made surreptitiously, as a deliberate abbreviation, from the memory of only two or three of the players. The cuts, it was thought, meant that its source must have been a version of the play made for touring, shortened for convenience of use by a smaller cast. On the other hand, if the transcribers were doing their job officially in the company's London playhouse, there is no reason why they could not have made reference to the playhouse manuscripts whenever they needed to. If this reading of the evidence has any validity, the text should show mishearings from dictation, mislineations by a scribe who was not told when the lines he was copying ended, and transpositions of words and phrases from other parts of the playhouse script either from his own or his reader's memory of performance. It should also show evidence of revision to cut parts, trim the longer speeches, and adapt the text where whole scenes were transposed or cut, or other changes to the staging demanded it. If the production of the Q text is related to a version of the F text altered for performance, it should also show signs of the transcribers' familiarity with the original manuscript. It does show signs of all of these characteristics.

The different levels or forms of adaptation merge in the Q text, so it is important to register the different kinds of evidence for each level. Two principal kinds of error can arise from the transcription process in Q. First, the 'reader', either speaking from his memory of the play in performance or reading from his playhouse manuscript, might misread what was in front of him. This is where some of the verbal substitutions, simplified adjectives, and omissions of lines or phrases might be generated. Secondly, the copyist might mishear what was said, and set it down wrongly. He might also misspell words that he misunderstood, misline his text, and just possibly omit some attendant features such as speech headings and stage directions.

The straightforward evidence of the kind of mishearings that come from transcribing a text given by dictation recur throughout Q. They include 1.32 'Sabeck', where Q conflates 'Sala' and 'Elbe'. Salic Law was given its name from the river called Sala or Salia. Here Sala is mistranscribed by infection from the other river's name. Simpler cases are 1.45 Q's 'the function' for F's 'defunction', 1.46 'Godly', for F's 'Idly', and in the same initial section Q's 'fate' for F's 'state' at 1.119. The same process generated 2.33 'talke' for 'take', 2.73 'tashan' for 'tertian', and perhaps 3.57 'quit in vs', for F's 'quick in us'. Here the Q version could be a misreading, but is more plausibly a mishearing. Other examples include 5.40 'demonstrated' for F's 'demonstratiue', 5.62 Q's 'hear' for F's ' him', 5.81 Q's 'musters' for F 'masters', 9.29 'packs' for F's 'pax', 9.34 'approach' for F's 'reproach', 9.79 'abraided' for 'vpbrayded', and 11.102 'chanceries' for F's 'chantries'. There are also signs of phonetic transcription by the scribe of a word he did not understand, such as Llewellyn's exclamation 'God's solud' at 11.30, and most conspicuously 11.77 'your a nasse'.

Other changes belong to the more usual forms of transmission error, where the text is misquoted or the scribe reverses a word or phrase. Not infrequently doublets were changed, either retaining one of the original words and substituting a fresh one, or simply reversing them. There are instances of this at 1.110 and 150, 3.4 and 19, and 5.6. Rather more radical instances of substitutions using words from other sections of the F text include 1.86 'coursing sneakers', where F's 'coursing snatchers' is the more technical term. Q's word comes from the subsequent line 109, where the Scots come 'sneaking'. Q similarly misapplies 'awe' at 1.121 for the rule of the bees, from Henry's use in F at line 158. Scene 19 also uses words from passages cut from the F text. In Burgundy's sole four-line speech at 19.10 'rub or bar' is taken from his F speech where he uses 'rub' in his eleventh line, and 'bar' in his fifth to mean the present scene, 'this Barre, and Royall enterview'.

The transcribers had for the most part a good ear for the verse. Even, and perhaps especially, if we accept that most of the mislineations came from the transcription process, the reader not bothering to give his copyist any explicit note of when each line ended, the passages where text was cut and adjustments had to be made, or where phrases were accidentally omitted or compressed, show a good sense of verse rhythms. F's two lines at 1.113, 'Since we haue lockes to safegard necessaries, / And pretty traps to catch the petty theeues', become the metrically perfect one line in Q, 'Since we haue trappes to catch the petty theeues'. Q compresses F's two lines into one, with only the loss of a paranomasia, and perfect metre. Most likely the pattern of transcription involved the reader dictating a full line of verse at a time to the transcriber. Such an agreed practice would explain almost all of the mislineations, including the handling of the numerous half-lines and the recording of all the prose scenes in lines of roughly verse length.

Confirmation that part of the transcription process was a direct reading of a written text is suggested by the number of misreadings that were generated by the peculiarities of the handwriting used in the source manuscript. The Q transcribers, for instance, made some of the d/e misreadings that are also characteristic of the F compositor. Q's 'combind' at 2.66 is a d/e misreading of the manuscript. At 13.13 F's 'contaminated' adds a 'd' to the basic word, where the metre demands the shorter but far less common form of the word. Q's 'contamuracke', which is metrically correct, looks very like a different misreading of the same word that misled the F compositor. Possibly Q's 'vilde', at 3.66, an interpolated word not in F, may have been misread for 'vile', although if so it was unlikely to have been one of the characteristic misreadings of the Shakespearean hand. More standard misreadings include Q's 'rackte' at 5.38, which must be a misreading of F's 'rakt' (raked), and 11.61 Q's 'gift', a misreading (more likely than a mishearing) for F's 'guilt'. Most clearly of all, at 3.8 the Q reader of the manuscript saw the word that in F is 'sits' as an address, 'sirs'. F's word was part of a standard phrasing for winds, possibly influenced by two uses of 'sit' in the Chorus to Act 2. The Q reader, seeing 'sits' as 'sirs', and not recognising it as a verb, consequently changed F's singular 'wind' by adding an elliptical verb 'is', freeing 'sirs' as an address, and making perfect grammatical sense of the line. That is not the sort of extended correction that a compositor misreading the manuscript would make. Nor, like other cases noted here, could it have been a mishearing by the copyist. The two transcribers, if they were using their memories to recall what they knew from performance, must have forgotten their scripts here.

It is possible that the process of making cuts in the longer speeches did something to the text that hampered the copyists as well. Almost every time a substantial number of lines disappear from a speech, the preceding two or more lines are mangled in some way. This can be seen most distinctly at 1.51, 116–18 and 218–19, 3.14, 53, 79–80, 94 and 105, and at 5.4–5. Mainly the changes simply try to keep good metre, but the scrawl noting the changes must have been difficult to decipher.

Other standard copying errors of substitution appear at 9.36, where Llewellyn addresses Pistol as 'Captain'. In F Pistol is always identified correctly by his rank. The Q copyist may have substituted the more correct title in his manuscript from Pistol's use of 'Captaine' to Llewellyn in the previous line. Similarly at 11.97 Q's 'hath' must be a copyist's error for F's 'haue', which makes better grammatical sense. At least one compositor error in F, the omission of a line, appears correctly in Q, in a section of heavy cuts and adaptations. Scene 12 line 42 was transferred by Q from the beginning of a section of re-lineated text, at line 30. The line that follows in Q is not in F, but has been adopted by editors since Malone as part of the F text, on the grounds that it was accidentally omitted in the F printing.

Re-lineation

If we accept that the mislineation, and the setting of prose as verse, was all a consequence of copying from dictation, the prose scenes certainly cannot be counted as a mark of the copyists' poor ears for verse. The verse sections indicate that the Q copyists knew their lines pretty well, and followed the verse with considerable care for line-ends and for a regular decasyllabic rhythm. They could be thrown off particularly in the vicinity of major cuts, producing extra-metrical syllables or short lines. Some damage may have been done to the manuscript copy when the cuts were first being accommodated. The transcription does appear to have tried to observe metrical patterns. Half-lines are used, especially to end speeches, and possibly on occasions for additional emphasis. In many places omitted words or phrases mess up the metre, but even then the copyists try to maintain or recover the iambic rhythm, as can be seen at 9.96 and 98. The first scene, all in verse, is a good example of how well they did the transcription of verse lines, since they were fairly fresh to their work, and Exeter, one of the transcribers, was a participant throughout the scene. Henry's speeches, here and elsewhere, have not generally been thought to be the products of a reporter from his memory of the part. Yet his speeches in the opening scene, and his last speech in scene 12, his reply to the French herald, are almost word-perfect. His main scene 12 speech is the same as the F version except for two cuts of three lines, where Q makes some small adjustments to admit them. The possibility that the revisers had access to a manuscript version of the part at least for this, Henry's longest speech in the Q version of the play, is very high.

In the opening scene, the Bishop's speech expounding his reading of the origin of Salic Law begins with a stumble at line 24. The reader, sounding the heavy caesura in the middle of line 23, which ends a sentence, allowed it to be as emphatic as a line-end. The Q transcriber therefore left it as a half-line, squeezing the remaining half-line into the next full line to make a single twelve-syllable line. That was the kind of error normal to the dictation process. The subsequent cutting of this speech – losing nine lines about Pharamond at line 47, two more about Hugh Capet usurping Charlemagne, and another ten about the lineage after line 50 – was all fitted into the metre with little need even to adjust the lines immediately adjacent to the cuts. In Q it stands as a ponderously formal speech, firmly rhythmical, making almost perfect sense of the argument and its long list of names and lineages, taking out only the most tangential sections, a perfectly coherent version of a lengthy and difficult-to-deliver set of verses.

Pistol's remarkable form of speech, with its Marlovian inversions and extreme vocabulary, is a comic trademark like's Nim's use of proverbial expressions, and the regional accents of the four captains. It has a unique mix of verse rhythms in what is essentially prose dialogue. George A Wright, in *Shakespeare's Metrical Art*, the most

Nim. I shall haue my eight shillings I wonne of you ✶
beating?
Pist. A noble shalt thou haue, and readie pay,
And liquor likewise will I giue to thee,
And friendshyp shall combind and brotherhood:
Ile liue by Nim as Nim shall liue by me:
Is not this iust? for I shall Sutler be
Vnto the Campe, and profit will occrue.
Nim. I shall haue my noble?
Pist. In cash most truly paid.
Nim. Why theres the humour of it.

Enter Hostes.

Hostes. As euer you came of men come in,
Sir Iohn poore soule is so troubled
With a burning tashan contigian feuer, tis wonderfull.
Pist. Let vs condoll the knight: for lambkins we will liue.
Exeunt omnes.

Enter Exeter and Gloster.

Glost. Before God my Lord, his Grace is too bold to trust
these traytors.
Exe. They shalbe apprehended by and by.
Glost. But the man that was his bedfellow
Whom he hath cloyed and graced with princely fauors.
That he should for a forraine purse, to sell
His Soueraignes life to death and treachery,
Exe. O the Lord of Masham.

Enter the King and three Lords.

King. Now sirs the windes faire, and we wil aboord;
My Lord of Cambridge, and my Lord of Masham,
And you my gentle Knight, giue me your thoughts,
Do you not thinke the power we beare with vs,
Will make vs conquerors in the field of France?
Masha. No doubt my Liege, if each man do his best.
Cam. Neuer

Cam. Neuer was Monarch better feared and loued then
is your maiestie.
Grey. Euen those that were your fathers enemies
Haue steeped their galles in honey for your sake.
King. We therefore haue great cause of thankfulnesse,
And shall forget the office of our hands:
Sooner then reward and merrit,
According to their cause and worthinesse.
Masha. So seruice shall with steeled sinewes shine,
And labour shall refresh it selfe with hope
To do your Grace incessant seruice.
King. Vncle of Exeter, enlarge the man
Committed yesterday, that rayled against our person,
We consider it was the heate of wine that set him on,
And on his more aduice we pardon him.
Masha. That is mercie, but too much securitie:
Let him bee punisht Soueraigne, least the example of
(him,
Breed more of such a kinde.
King. O let vs yet be mercifull.
Cam. So may your highnesse, and punish too.
Grey. You shew great mercie if you giue him life,
After the taste of his correction.
King. Alas your too much care and loue of me
Are the heauy orisons gainst the poore wretch,
If litle faults proceeding on distemper should not bee
(winked at,
How should we stretch our eye, when capitall crimes,
Chewed, swallowed and disgested, appeare before vs:
Well yet enlarge the man, tho Cambridge and the rest
In their deare loues, and tender preseruation of our states,
Would haue him punisht.
Now to our French causes,
Who are the late Commissioners?
Cam. Me one my Lord, your highnesse bad me aske for
it to day.
Masha. So

B 3

A page from the first quarto. Note the consistent lineation as verse in the scenes using comic prose

sensitive of recent studies of Shakespeare's metre, calls Pistol's speech 'strange me-
tered prose' and 'hapless iambic prose'. He argues that 'we have no reason to believe
that any of his lines are verse, except for their relentlessly iambic character.'[1] In this
edition, as in the NCS text, Pistol's lines are set as prose. The Q compositor tried to set
Pistol's lines, like everyone else's, as verse, by-passing the confusion over his lineation
which the revisers and the F printer shared equally. In the first of the Eastcheap scenes,
it was probably the compositor who was most confused, since he set the initial dialogue
between Bardolph and Nim as prose, then changed the whole scene to verse at Pistol's
entry with Mistress Quickly. All the speeches after that are set with initial capitals as
unjustified lines, approximating to verse, and in the rest of the play their lines are all
set as verse.

Premeditated revisions

There is evidence for much more careful drafting of the Q text than the assumption
that it is 'corrupt' has allowed till now. Mostly the cuts to the formal speeches were
made sensibly, and probably fairly early in the revision process. What needs to be
noted as evidence for the authoritative character of the alterations to the F text is how
relevant were the changes where for instance a passage in F is inserted into a different
section of Q, the practical nature of some changes, and the consistency with which the
smaller changes of name, pronouns and other details were included.

The question of those cuts which generated the three cases where characters exited
and immediately had to re-enter has been dealt with above. The Q text's revisions are
least faithful to F not in the cutting process itself but in the consequent adjustments,
particularly where the cuts are used to shorten a scene. On the whole, the major cuts,
such as in Henry's longer speeches, had little effect on the accuracy of the transcription, but the comic dialogues, including Henry's French exchanges with the princess,
were regularly shortened and the sequence of the jokes altered in the process. The
comic scenes were curtailed and altered much more than the verse scenes, where the
cutting was careful and relatively sparse.

Above all there is the question whether the Q revisers ever had access to the original
manuscript to check their texts, and whether the manuscript they consulted was in fact
already a later version of the text than the one used to print F. Henry's longest speech,
to Montjoy in scene 12, is a case in point. The Q version cuts only two small sections
of three lines from F's thirty-seven, and, apart from the lines adjacent to the cuts,
reproduces them more precisely than almost any other passage in the play. It copies
even the most awkward lines and odd words exactly. At 12.75, for instance, Q and
F agree on an unusual word, both spelling it 'crasing'. Two lines later, at 12.77, Q
reproduces more precisely than usual F's awkward version of the line, which is often
altered by editors. Most remarkable of all, though, are two rare words in Q which
replace much more ordinary terms in F. Q's 'leno' at 13.11 is a rare and sophisticated
non-English version of F's 'Pander', used twice by Nashe, but otherwise hardly

---

[1] George A. Wright, *Shakespeare's Metrical Art*, Berkeley: University of California Press, 1988, pp. 110–11.

known.[1] Another rare Q word replacing an ordinary one in F is 1.134, 'caning'. A regional word from the fifteenth and sixteenth centuries (OED v.2), its meaning, the scum or dross formed in mis-brewed ale that has gone sour, is a much more vivid image for the activity of the beehive's drones than F's 'yawning'. If we follow the standard editorial practice and prefer the rarer words as more likely to be Shakespeare's than the more commonplace, the conclusion on this evidence must be that Shakespeare introduced a few changes to his copy that postdate the manuscript used to print F, and that some at least of these revisions appear in the Q text. Eliminating the Dauphin from Agincourt may not have been the only authorised revision that appears in Q.

With these striking exceptions, it can be said that in general the players as revisers of the F text, or their Q scribes, consistently reduced F's more colourful and unusual adjectives to something simpler. In the exclamatory French scene 8, for instance, 'surreyned' and 'roping' become 'swollen' and 'frozen' respectively, and 'Albion' becomes 'England'. Even Pistol's extravagant lexis underwent that process at times. At 9.31 QI offers the ordinary 'death' in place of F's 'Hempe'. Normalising the vocabulary so consistently in this way makes all the more striking the existence of Q's 'caning' and 'leno'.

Re-assignments of parts

Besides the likelihood that it was the players who consistently simplified the more exotic words in the F text, the most obvious matter to undergo revision between the delivery of the manuscript that was eventually used to print F and the preparation of the Q copy was the removal of the Dauphin from the Agincourt scenes. The speeches that F assigns in Acts 3 and 4 to the Dauphin are re-assigned to Bourbon in Q. In scene 10 both Orleans and Gebon identify him by name as the Duke of Bourbon. The Q text also, possibly through confusion with the tradition that Nashe mentions from the old play where the Dauphin had to kneel in submission to Henry at the end, turns Burgundy into Bourbon for the entry direction for the last scene, although the text names him as Burgundy.

Apart from that slip, the care with which the Dauphin's removal was accomplished seems to be reflected in some consistent revisions made in the first scene, where Henry receives the insult of the tennis balls. In F his response is purely personal. He uses not the royal 'we' but the personal 'I' throughout his speech in reply to the ambassador, insisting that he personally will 'venge me as I may', and that his appeal to God is a personal one. Q throughout this scene makes him use the royal plural. At first this seems merely a formal use of the language of majesty, but changing the threats he makes to the ambassador into 'we' invokes the support of the English lords present with him, and suggests that the whole nation has a single mind to invade France. A similar change is made in Scene 3, where Henry confronts the conspirators. Q replaces F's 'person' in his speech at 3.42 as the subject to be protected with the word 'state'.

---

[1] See Gary Taylor, 'Shakespeare's Leno: *Henry V* IV.v.14', *NQ* 224 (1979), 117–18.

The same Q insistence on Henry using the nationalistic plural appears in scene 16, when he speaks to Montjoy.

This may, of course, simply reflect the standard speech-habits of royalty, because something similar happens to the French king. Where in F he urges the princes to 'look you strongly arm to meet' Henry, in Q he uses the royal first-person plural to say that France does believe Henry to be strong, and is strongly arming 'to prevent the foe'. Q's version is more emphatic, firmly distancing the French king from the Dauphin. On the other hand, for all the royal decorum, in the same scene at 5.22 the F's messenger's line announcing the arrival of an ambassador from England to the French court is taken by the onstage Constable, an economy which makes Exeter march in without any ceremony or formal announcement. Possibly that was intended. The absence of stage directions calling for the trumpet signals normal with royal entries and exits may be a similar curtailment, although there may be a different explanation for that. If the Q text was made not for performance use – the company already had the revised script from which this text was being copied – but for the press, as a reader's text, that would explain quite a few of the other oddities in the Q text, such as the three exits where some of the characters who leave then immediately re-enter to begin the next scene. In a text meant for readers, not for the theatre, stage directions noting musical signals might have been thought a redundancy.

But such changes are hard to separate from the evidence for deliberate revision to make a simpler and shorter playing text. The massive trimming of the Harfleur scenes, with the complete elimination of Henry's thirty-four lines of the 'Once more unto the breach' speech, and of the scene with Jamy and MacMorris, plus the thirty-five lines cut from Henry's threatening speech before Harfleur was done thoroughly and consistently. Bardolph's take-up from Henry's speech, his shouted 'On, on, on, on, on, to the breach, to the breach', is cut, and he says nothing at all in the Q version. The revisers shortened the whole Harfleur experience, making all the toings and froings into a single scene, taking out any hint that Henry's actions in the siege might have failed, either in getting his troops through the breach, or by using the F 'Scaling Ladders' for the assault. There is a confident re-design behind these alterations, a shift of emphasis away from the first military struggle and its setbacks onto the total success of Agincourt. The one scene that is not seriously truncated in the Q version of this act is the introduction of Princess Katherine. Eliminating the Chorus to this act cut out his reference to the French king offering Henry his daughter, and the assertion that, despite what is proclaimed in Act 5 of both versions, 'the offer likes not'.

The underlying emphasis of the changes is of course to intensify Henry's heroism, and to play down the setbacks to his campaign. From the opening where the whole scene between the two bishops is cut, so that the exposition of the case for Henry's title to the French crown becomes less an expedient tactic on Canterbury's part than an open statement of a good legal case, through Henry's royal 'we' and the later elimination of references to his rejection of Falstaff, the Q text affirms the depersonalised rightness of the war.

Another instance of Q's radical trimming, and one where the manuscript behind the F version is somehow involved, is the cutting of Henry's ceremony speech

and Erpingham's interruption of it from 4.1. Immediately after Henry's debate
with the soldiers in scene 11, Q has a stage direction for Henry to enter with Gloster
and Erpingham. This is a nonsense, since Henry is already on stage, Gloster
arrives sixteen lines later to call Henry to the battle, and Erpingham was cut out of
the Q text altogether. The stage direction in Q must be a survival from an earlier
manuscript draft, set at the beginning of 4.3 in F, where the full stage direction
reads

> *Enter Gloucester,Bedford,Exeter,Erpingham*
> *with all his Hoast: Salisbury,and*
> *Westmerland.*

The similarity between this and Q's '*Enter the King, Gloster, Epingam, and Attendants*'
makes a powerful case for the revisers of the Q text being familiar with the manuscript
behind the F text, and ignoring or forgetting the version behind Q that represented
what they knew as the stage version. That may have happened early in the adaptation
process, when the concern was to cut the number of parts, a process involving
consultation of an earlier version much closer to the F manuscript. That such consultation with a manuscript close to the author's original could take place is confirmation
that the revisers did their work in the playhouse, with total authority.

Cutting the number of parts in Q raises the question of doubling. There is good
evidence that the practice of doubling parts to enable a fixed number of players to
perform any specific play was well developed by 1599. In the few years of London
staging up to 1594 plays were written for large casts, of fifteen or more.[1] After that the
number shrank, and Scott McMillin has produced good evidence from the quartos of
the Chamberlain's players produced betweeen 1600 and 1608 for a maximum of eleven
speaking parts.[2] He makes the point that when a text is shortened, the doubling of
parts is actually made more difficult. That, besides reducing the likelihood that such
texts were ever shortened specifically for touring in the country, reduces the importance of the practicalities of doubling in the Q version of the play as against the F's
needs.

In practical terms, the reduction in the number of roles in the Q text can have had
almost no effect on the calculations over doubling. It simply reduces the number
of named nobles on stage. None of the name-changes in Q show much concern
for historical accuracy. Replacing Westmorland took out a figure who was not at
Agincourt according to Holinshed, and substituted not a known historical presence
such as Oxford (who is named in the older *Famous Victories of Henry V*, published in
1598), but the more evocative and less historical name of Warwick. This may have
been another of the author's revisions, since Warwick has a small walk-on part in the
F text. Reducing the two names of Henry's brothers Bedford and Gloucester to one
was a simpler economy. Reducing the number of French nobles was another. The
parts cut completely, notably Westmorland, Bedford, Erpingham, the French Queen,

---

[1] See Gurr, 'The Chimera of Amalgamation', *Theatre Research International* 18 (1993), 85–93.
[2] 'Casting the *Hamlet* Quartoes: The Limit of Eleven', in *The 'Hamlet' First Published (Q1, 1603): Origins, Form, Intertextualities*, ed. Thomas Clayton, Newark, NJ: University of Delaware Press, 1992, pp. 179–94.

Macmorris and Jamy, were made principally to reduce the number of small speaking parts. The net result was a slight reduction in the number of roles that had to be doubled, but no overall change in the number of players that either text required for performance.[1]

Q's use of the cuts from F

A more complex matter in the evolution of the Q version from the F manuscript is the use in Q of words that appear to come from the F scenes that were cut. It has some bearing on the reasons for the general pattern of changes. The references in Q 1.3 to matters 'touching . . . France', for instance, may have taken their initial wording from the opening scene where the Archbishop tells his colleague that he has to speak to the king on causes 'As touching France' (F.1.1.79). Since it occurs in the three lines altered to accommodate the cut of F's first scene, it may well have appeared there in the initial process of adjusting the text from the longer version. If so, it was most likely an official if not an authorised alteration, and almost certainly one made by somebody possessing knowledge of the full F version. Something similar may have happened in scene 11, which begins with Henry appearing in disguise, and enacting the encounter in disguise with Pistol, but then going to meet the English soldiers as if he were enacting the 'little touch of Harry in the night' that the fourth Chorus boasts of.

Amongst these changes, the evidence for the Q version radically altering the staging is substantial, but not much has been made of the fact that it is also coherent. Commentators have noted that the scenes before the battle are trimmed in Q. Incongruity has been noted in the transfer of the final couplet from a scene in F cut out of Q, about the sun being high, to the end of scene 10, at dawn. That this was a purposive change is indicated by other small changes that marked the speeding-up of time in the following scene, for instance 11.29 where F's 'heare' becomes Gower's 'heard' in Q, as if the noise of the French was a feature of the night that is now past, and a few lines later where F's talk about the soldiers not seeing the end of the next day turns into 'this day' ending. The adaptation of F into Q appears in a number of ways to have been not only a matter of shortening the text but of altering its speed.

The question how purposive were the revisions of the staging in Q is complicated by the number of stage directions that Q omits. There are certainly some necessary stage directions missing in Q, particularly exits. Nor are there any directions for trumpet-calls or military drum signals. The flourishes that should accompany a royal entry and exit are omitted from both scene 1 and scene 5, for instance. The intrusive entry for the lords when Henry is at prayer in scene 11, has already been considered. Some of the lost stage directions may have disappeared in the cutting process. At 18.33.1, for instance, Q gives no exit for Gower, although Pistol's last speech is spoken solo. Gower's last ten-line diatribe to Pistol in F is cut, and, if the copyist here was making use of the F manuscript, the cut must have taken his '*Exit*' direction at the end of it

---

[1] The idea that companies on tour were smaller than they were when playing in London has no evidence to support it. See David Bradley, *From Text to Performance in the Elizabethan Theatre: Preparing the Play for the Stage*, Cambridge, 1992, pp. 58–74.

with the rest. The entry direction for scene 19 names the French princess as '*Queene* Katherine'. Q's text omits Queen Isabel, who is named in F's entry direction, and has a speaking part. Once again, the '*Queene*' in Q may be a survival from the original stage direction that a manuscript copyist or the transcribers failed to cut. The most likely reason for such imperfect adjustments to the stage directions, including the elimination of the stage directions about trumpet-calls, has been noted above.

Another hint that the manuscript from which F was printed lies fairly directly behind Q's reconstruction comes with the switch of scenes 13 and 14. The reversal makes Pistol leave at the end of scene 14 and re-enter immediately following the king and his nobles for scene 15. At the end of scene 13, immediately preceding scene 14 in F, the stage direction specifies '*Alarum*', the only direct indication of battle in the F version. It is followed by the direction opening this scene, '*Enter the King and his trayne, with Prisoners*'. Q's version, which comes after scene 14 with Pistol and his prisoner, marks no sound of battle, and supplies an entry for '*the King and his Nobles, Pistoll*'. This, a consequence of Q's reversal of F's scenes 13 and 14, requires Pistol to leave and immediately re-enter.

Verbal alterations for consistency

The verbal alterations in Q are also for the most part coherent and consistent. At 8.18–19, where the French king's twenty-line speech reciting the great names of the French nobles is cut entirely in Q, along with the Constable's four-line response, the whole cut is replaced with two invented lines summoning the French herald. That leaves the French king's order to the Dauphin to stay with him as the last and therefore most emphatic word in the scene. Even the comic scene 14 between Pistol and M. Le Fer is changed consistently. At line 12, Q's French differs from F's not just in its inaccuracy. It simplifies the question and answer at 15–16. The Frenchman's next speech is a very broad paraphrase of F, losing the reference to pleading on his knees, calling Pistol a '*grand captaine*' instead of a '*Chevalier*', and specifying a ransom of only fifty '*écus*', a sum the Boy multiplies tenfold. The Boy's last soliloquy to the audience, with its anticipation of the attack on the boys and the baggage, and its account of Nim's death along with Bardolph, is also cut. The whole scene is shorter and tighter, but it lacks none of the original fun, adds the Boy's inflation of the size of the ransom offered, and deletes the ominous hint that the Boy is about to die as Bardolph and Nim have. In F he derides them as he had done before in scene 6, while announcing their deaths, all references to which are cut from Q.

Similar adjustments appear to be made to Llewellyn's part. Besides the increased use of his distinctive catchphrases, such as 'look you', which match the redoubling of such phrases among the comics, like Nim's 'and there's the humour of it', Q strengthens some of Llewellyn's other verbal habits. In Scene 9.12 after describing his first meeting with Pistol, he says 'I do not know how you call him.' When he finishes praising him, Gower asks 'How do you call him?', and Llewellyn promptly answers 'His name is Ancient Pistol.' Such a question and its answer so soon after saying he does not know the name is an anomaly. Llewellyn's line about not knowing his name is not in F, so in that text the question and answer are more fitting. On the other hand, Llewellyn elsewhere does forget names twice, at 16.9 (Macedon) and 32 (Falstaff), in both texts. The apparent contradiction in Q may simply have been an intensification of one of his mental traits.

Shakespeare's changes or the players'?

It is impossible to be sure who made almost any of the deliberate changes to the manuscript used for the F text, before the play reached the stage and its Q version. Evidence for the author changing his mind is in the epilogue to *2 Henry IV*, also printed in 1600, which asserts that the next play will have 'Sir John in it'. The removal of Falstaff was part of an adjustment process made long before the removal of the Dauphin from Agincourt and its consequence. Conceivably, given the disappointment of losing Falstaff, Q1's titlepage can be seen to advertise its Ancient Pistol as a tacit compensation for the disappearance. The 1602 quarto of *The Merry Wives of Windsor*, also printed by Creede, advertised itself as filled with 'the swaggering vaine of Auncient *Pistoll*, and Corporall *Nym*', in a similar manner, almost as a reminder of the Eastcheap fun of *Henry V*, even though *Merry Wives* did have Sir John in it.

It is true that many of the changes visible in Q made the play more simply the heroic story of Henry's victory than the F version allows him to be. The loss of the Choruses, and therefore of the distinct instances where the audience hears things said in praise of Henry that the following act calls in question, is unreliable evidence. More clear-cut as evidence for simplifying the heroic side are the cuts in Q's second scene where Falstaff's sickness is introduced. Q omits all three references to it being a consequence of Henry turning him away. We can only guess whether it was Shakespeare who made these cuts, or the three players whose lines they were, or the company adapters, or the transcribers of the quarto manuscript.

Practical changes that quickened and simplified the action include the Harfleur scenes and 5.61, where in F the French king gives a temporising reply before the Dauphin is allowed to respond. Q transfers his reply to later, and makes the Dauphin pick up Exeter's invitation at once. Simpler streamlining is to be seen at, for instance, 17.7.1, where in F Warwick and Gloster enter first, followed by Henry and Exeter five lines later. Warwick's initial demand to know what is happening disappears along with Llewellyn's four-line reply, so that all four characters can enter together.

Some of the more considered changes may well have been authorised. The transfer of Exeter's parting shot to the French king in scene 5, for instance, into the king's own warning words at the beginning of the scene, is a sensible adjustment. Although it loses the anticipation of the action at Harfleur which follows, it adds urgency to the French council's debate. The elimination of the opening scene, with its revelation of Canterbury's ulterior motive for urging war on Henry, led naturally to the cut in Q from the Bishop's speech of the six lines containing his offer of funds for the war, which in F serves as a reminder of the Archbishop's duplicity. That was at least consistent with Q's general tendency to minimise any doubts about the war.

Other practical changes in Q include a one-line addition by Exeter at the beginning of scene 3. His four-line account of the treachery by Scrope, Lord Masham, Henry's closest friend, is transferred to Gloster, and the Q Exeter merely contributes a line identifying who he is referring to – 'Oh, the lord of Masham'. It is a neat and sensible adjustment, which serves not only as a consequence of deleting Westmorland's part and developing Bedford's lines for Gloster, but to clarify which character they are alluding to. It also supports Henry's entry with the other two conspirators immediately after, when he names and identifies them one by one. Q uses only the name 'Masham' for Lord Scroop throughout, cutting every use of his other name, at lines 41, 48 and 84. Since it also gives Exeter his extra line specifying the name as Masham, this must be part of the routine process of tidying the original copy by simplifying the names. A more doubtful case from the same scene is the two adjacent uses in F of 'much', by Gray and by Henry. It is at least conceivable that the author decided to alter one of the uses to avoid pointless repetition, with the result that, by one of the kinds of adjustment that makes overkill, both were crossed out.

Many of the more seemingly casual alterations appear in the comic scenes. They provide not only intensification of the various characters' catchphrases but deliberate new jokes or phrases, like Pistol's obscene reference to the Hostess's 'bugle bow' at 4.34, and his reiteration of 'Couple gorge' at the end of scene 15. Nim uses 'and there's the humour of it' eight times in Q to the five more varied forms of F. A similar shift occurs in *The Merry Wives of Windsor*, where the Q gives him five such phrases to none in the Folio text. Llewellyn uses his oaths more frequently in Q, and develops several verbal idioms that hardly qualify as catchphrases, but nonetheless characterise him with precision. In scenes 16 and 17 he several times starts sentences with the conditional 'an if', particularly when addressing Henry. 'An if it shall please your Majesty' recurs six times in Q, and once it is applied to pleasing God, while it is never used in F. Q does lose some nuances in the locutions written for Llewellyn, notably his use of superbly pedantic polysyllables like 'magnanimous as *Agamemnon*', but his colourful speech, contrasted as it is to Pistol's bombast, grows into the strongest single feature of Q's version of the comic scenes.

How many of the changes in the comic scenes were designed as deliberate shifts in emphasis is not easy to see. Cutting the references to Henry's responsibility for Falstaff dying is one. The deletion of any mention of Nim's death is another, but the reference to Bardolph's, in Henry's presence, remains. The conflict between Pistol and Llewellyn also remains, but the nuance in F that Henry's order to kill the prisoners loses Pistol the chance of an 'egregious' ransom is forgotten in favour of the glee of his approving 'Couple gorge!' exclamation at the end of scene 15. Pistol's gratuitous admission to that scene, and his gruesome exclamation at the end when Henry orders the prisoners to be killed, has prompted a lot of debate since Gary Taylor first suggested that the reason for F's stage direction at TLN 2484 where the king's train enters '*with Prisoners*' was so that they could have their throats cut on stage.[1] It is certain that this was a designed change from F, where the order to kill the prisoners is framed not in Pistol's reaction but in the mistaken and misleading reaction by Gower

[1] See Taylor, 'Shakespeare's Leno', 117–18.

and Llewellyn. Whether the change was initiated by Shakespeare is a matter for speculation.

Stage history

Apart from a performance at court on 7 January 1605, no early records survive of the play's performance in any version. Besides some corrections of the *Henry V* story embodied in the text of *1 Sir John Oldcastle* by the Globe's neighbours playing at the Rose in late 1599, a few other echoes of the text do exist in contemporary writing that suggest it was well known in 1600 and 1601. The intriguing question is which version.

The references to *Henry V* in *1 Sir John Oldcastle* are clear-cut. They made a great point of featuring the mistakes the Shakespeare company had made in staging the first Falstaff play, *1 Henry IV*, with his original name, Sir John Oldcastle. Oldcastle was a Protestant hero in Foxe's *Book of Martyrs*, and his descendant was Lord Chamberlain for eight months from August 1596, while the play was still a major hit. By 1599 the company at the Rose, who had recently become reluctant neighbours to the Globe company, were facing up to the consequences of their main competitor opening only fifty yards away. In September 1599 their impresario Philip Henslowe commissioned a pair of plays called *Sir John Oldcastle* from four writers, Michael Drayton, Richard Hathway, Antony Munday and Robert Wilson. The object was plainly to call attention to its new neighbour's former trouble with the name Oldcastle. Henslowe paid over the odds for the play that put the Chamberlain's Men's record straight, and added another ten pounds 'as a gefte' when it was staged, at the end of October or the beginning of November 1599.[1] He later paid Dekker to revise it for performance at court. The Shakespeare company had dropped the name of Oldcastle and apologised for their error years before, in the epilogue to *2 Henry IV* ('for Oldcastle died a martyr, and this is not the man'), but with the Globe newly established on the Rose's doorstep the Rose company thought it too good an opportunity to miss. John Weever, a poet connected to Shakespeare in obscure ways, did a similar job of retrieving Oldcastle's reputation by writing a life of Oldcastle in 1599,[2] a poem published in 1601 as *A Mirror for Martyrs*. His verses however did not rub the mistake in as the play did.

The Rose play was written to present the martyr's life chiefly in relation to his king, Henry V. In consequence it sought to correct not only the story of Oldcastle (usually called in the play Lord Cobham, his title through marriage), but the historical errors in the Shakespeare plays up to and including *Henry V*. It begins with a reproving prologue about presenting none of the '*forg'd invention former time defac'd*', but it

---

[1] See Carol Chillington Rutter, *Documents of the Rose Playhouse*, Manchester, 1984, p. 169.

[2] Weever's dedicatory letter says that it 'some two yeares agoe was made fit for the Print'. This suggests that he wrote it not long after the original fracas in 1596, when the name in the play was first changed from Oldcastle to Falstaff. It may have been an early attempt at correcting Oldcastle's public image from the damage Shakespeare did it. The poem shows knowledge of *Julius Caesar*, staged in 1599, since its fourth stanza speaks of '*Brutus* speach, that *Caesar* was ambitious' (A3v), and it also shows familiarity with *Richard II* on stage ('So *Bullingbrooke* unto the gazers eyes / Riseth in *Richards* royall chaire of state', C3v), but it has no echoes of *Henry V*.

nonetheless makes substantial use of some of the successes in the Shakespeare plays for its own purposes. Its writers transferred the Falstaff characteristics and some Pistollian oaths to 'Sir John Wrotham', a man who describes himself in soliloquy as 'A priest in shew, but in plaine termes, a theefe'. He has a lover called Doll, robs the disguised king and later gambles and loses his winnings back to him. Henry identifies himself through a French crown which Wrotham breaks in two, as a gage like Williams's glove. That prompts a joke about 'crackt french crownes' (line 1537).[1] The game of cross-references is emphasised when this Sir John complains to Henry that in the past he was robbed by Falstaff along with Peto and Poins. Other echoes of *Henry V* include a lengthy correction of F's conspiracy scene, 2.2., explaining the place of Cambridge as Henry's rival in the English lineage. The Rose play also has an Irish thief with an Irish accent and clothing, and two other verbal references besides the French crowns, both of which have a bearing on the question which version of the play was put on stage at the Globe in 1599.

The first of the verbal references is *Oldcastle*'s list of the nobles accompanying Henry as he faces the Lollard rebellion in London, while preparing to invade France. We are told that 'Your noble uncle Exeter is there, / Your brother Gloucester and my Lord of Warwicke' (1468–9). These are the chief names of Henry's nobles as they appear in the Q text. *Oldcastle* makes no mention of F's Bedford or Westmorland. From this it might seem that the compilers of the Rose play heard only the Q text. But the other verbal echo is in the names Cambridge, Scroope and Gray, the conspirators. They meet in the seventh scene of *Oldcastle* to discuss their plans with the French envoy, Chartres, and to rehearse Cambridge's claim to the throne which is so tightly suppressed in both Shakespeare's F version and in Q. The possibly distinctive name is *Oldcastle*'s Scroope, the main title given him in Foxe's story. Whereas Q uniformly changes Scroope into 'my Lord of Masham', in *1 Sir John Oldcastle* he is consistently 'Lord Scroope'. So one of these two pieces of evidence seems to indicate that only the quarto version was on stage for the Henslowe writers in 1599, while the other seems to suggest that, assuming they were not making too close a use of their alternative source in Foxe's book, they had probably heard a version closer to the Folio.

The Irishman's presence, and his distinctive clothing, includes a pair of 'strouces' which may relate to the 'strait strossers' that the French refer to in the F text, and which might have distinguished Macmorris on stage. Such an otherwise randomly generated character in a play so directly stimulated by *Henry V* at the Globe may argue for Macmorris's presence in the staged version of NCS 3.3. as an indication that it was the F text of the play that was staged in 1599. There are not many other comic Irishmen in the plays of this time, although it is a nice question whether the rebellion of 1598 might have either stimulated or inhibited such presentations on the contemporary stages. Given the regular reference to Shakespeare's play in the *Oldcastle* text, it does seem likely that they had seen enough of Captain Macmorris to prompt their presentation of an Irish thief. It may just be, of course, that the copying went the other way,

---

[1] Quotations and line references are from the Malone Society Reprints edition, 1908, ed. Percy Simpson.

and that the addition of Macmorris went with Scots Jamy as a late insertion in the F manuscript.[1] That is less likely, if only because Macmorris was written in from the start in F, and his presence and his personality are basic to his confrontation with Llewellyn, whereas Jamy was a distinctly odd addendum. The stage presentation of an Irishman as a thief would have been popular in London in 1598–9. On the other hand, to present him as a Captain in Henry's army at such a time, however comic his role, was almost as peculiar an inclusion as Scottish Jamy. The deletion of both from the staged text would have been sensible for different political reasons.

All three of the other echoes, one each from 1600, 1601 and 1602, may indicate some familiarity with the play in performance, although apart from a faint possibility about the first none of them affirms which version of the play the early playgoers heard. The first of the possible echoes appeared in Christopher Middleton's poem *The Legend of Humphrey Duke of Glocester*. Prefaced by complimentary poems from Michael Drayton, and Robert Allott, author of *England's Parnassus*, also published in 1600, it is a history in 184 six-line stanzas of the 'good Duke Humphrey' who figures with the downfall of his wife in Shakespeare's *1 Henry VI*. Its fifth stanza ends with a phrase which is the most tantalising of the three apparent echoes, because it is the same as a phrase in the Folio text's Prologue. The stanza says

> What time this land disquieted with broyles,
> Wearied with wars and spent for want of rest,
> Save her adjoyning neighbours free from th'spoyles,
> Wherewith her selfe, her selfe had disposest
> Of peace and plenty, which men most desire,
> And in their steeds brought famine, sword, and fire. (B1v)

The seventh line of *Henry V*'s Prologue in the Folio version has the last four words in exactly the same order. Conceivably, therefore, Middleton had recently seen the play and heard the Prologue. There is, however, nothing else in the poem's eleven hundred lines that resembles either version of the play even remotely, except possibly for a line in stanza 39, 'Now Lyon-like he forrages the land', which could be a faint echo of Q 1.75's 'Foraging', F's 'Forrage in' (TLN 257). There is, though, another and more likely source for the four words of the Prologue. In Act 4 of *1 Henry VI*, Talbot, threatening the French on the walls at Bordeaux, speaks of his 'three attendants, / Leane Famine, quartering Steele, and climbing Fire' (TLN 1960–1). Shakespeare's own Prologue was probably a recollection of this speech, since it follows the same sequence of famine, sword and fire, whereas the F source, Holinshed, has 'blood, fire & famine'. Middleton, whose whole poem is based on the story of Duke Humphrey from Shakespeare's older play, may have had the same recollection, and compressed it in the identical way.

The other two echoes are of sections of the play that exist in both the Folio and the

---

[1] It has been pointed out that the Jamy section of 3.3. can be cut cleanly out of the F text with almost no other change. See Keith Brown, 'Historical Context and *Henry V*', *Cahiers Elisabethaines* 29 (1986), 77–85. That might be a mark of Jamy's late inclusion in the play. Macmorris, however, was integrated early on. His omission from the final section of the play probably indicates another late change of mind, like the removal of the Dauphin.

Quarto versions, and are of words far less in common currency. In *Poetaster* (1601) Jonson gave his Crispinus, being hauled off to prison, the plea 'do not exhale me thus'.[1] A rare word, the sort of extravagance that Crispinus shares with Pistol, it very likely echoes Pistol's exclamation to Nim at 2.40. The third echo is even more positive. Nicholas Breton's *A Poste with a Packet of Mad Letters* of 1602 is a compilation of wittily fictional letters, printed in blackletter, mainly composed of calculated insults and their replies. It includes a reply from a 'coy Dame' responding to one 'of scorne' from a rejected suitor, which begins with these words:

> Maister Swash, it is not your hustie rustie, can make me afraid of your bigge lookes: for I sawe the plaie of Ancient *Pistoll*, where a craking coward was well cudgeled for his knauery: your railing is so neare the Rascall, that I am almost ashamed to bestow so good a name as the Rogue vppon you . . . (CI)

The letter which this answers is phrased in a railing and swaggering style, vaguely Pistol's vein, whose 'so good a name' was pronounced 'Pizzle', a word for the penis. Llewellyn's cudgelling of Pistol in the penultimate scene was evidently one of the more memorable features of the early stagings, since it also registered in Compositor B's memory, and made him augment it when he set the Q3 text in 1619. These two echoes confirm the idea that the play was popular for a while after 1599, but they do not provide absolute confirmation that the version everyone knew from the staging was Q, likely though it is. In any case, at any time from mid-1600 on they could have known the play by reading it in Q's version.

[1] *Jonson* IV.245. Herford and Simpson gloss 'exhale' at IX.554 as 'to drag away'.

NOTE ON THE TEXT

This edition is based on the first text of Shakespeare's *Henry V* to appear in print, the quarto of 1600. It is a companion volume to this editor's NCS version of the play, which is based on the First Folio text. Spellings are modernised, and abbreviations regularised roughly in accordance with the NCS practice. The spelling of characters' names largely follows those adopted for the NCS edition, except for 'Gloster', where the version common to both Elizabethan and modern pronunciation is used. Punctuation largely follows that in the quarto, except where the syntax demands some clarification. Any other substantive alterations from the Q copy, and all emendations, are registered in the collation. Where it has seemed necessary to add a stage direction, it has been enclosed in square brackets.

Elisions are marked with an apostrophe, where the metre demands it. All *-ed* endings of words are elided, except where an accent marks the pronounced vowel. The familiar basic beat of the verse, the ten-syllable line of five stresses or rising iambs, has been accepted as the standard metre. The Q text not infrequently gets this metre wrong, but the corrections here have all been recorded in the commentary notes. In most cases, the common practice of modern editors, making one speech ending in a half-line into a full verse line by linking it to the half-line which launches the next speech, has been ignored here.

The collation supplies the authority for the text used in this edition immediately after the lemma. Other significant readings follow, in the chronological order of their first appearance. Appendices 1 and 2, pp. 117–20 below, supply examples of the larger changes, including those to the verse lineation.

Because Q's version of the play was created as a text without breaks of any kind, this edition follows the Q sequence of scenes, numbering them in succession with no reference to the division into acts which appears in the Folio (wrongly), or to the more complete act and scene divisions in the NCS and other editions. In case this impedes any quick cross-referencing to the Folio version in the NCS and other editions, each of the Q edition's scenes is related to its equivalent in the NCS edition in a Textual Note.

The Chronicle History of Henry the Fifth

LIST OF CHARACTERS

In order of appearance (speech headings denoted by capitals)

KING HENRY V
Earl of EXETER
BISHOP of Canterbury
Earl of CLARENCE
French AMBASSADOR
NIM
BARDOLPH
Ancient PISTOL
Hostess QUICKLY
BOY
Earl of GLOSTER
Earl of CAMBRIDGE
Lord Scroop of MASHAM
Sir Thomas GRAY
FRENCH KING
Duke of BOURBON
DAUPHIN
CONSTABLE of France
Captain GOWER
Captain LLEWELLYN
GOVERNOR of Harfleur
Princess KATHERINE
Lady ALICE, her maid
French HERALD, Mountjoy
Duke of ORLEANS
GEBON
3 SOLDIERS
Earl of SALISBURY
Earl of WARWICK
FRENCH man
English HERALD
Soldiers, Attendants, Messenger

THE CHRONICLE HISTORY
of Henry the Fifth: with his battle fought at Agincourt in France.
Together with Ancient Pistol

[1] *Enter* KING HENRY, EXETER, 2 BISHOPS, CLARENCE, *and other Attendants*

EXETER Shall I call in th'ambassadors, my liege?
KING Not yet, my cousin, till we be resolved
        Of some serious matters touching us and France.
BISHOP God and his angels guard your sacred throne,
        And make you long become it.   5
KING Sure we thank you. And good my lord, proceed
        Why the law Salic which they have in France
        Or should or should not stop us in our claim;
        And God forbid, my wise and learned lord,
        That you should fashion, frame or wrest the same.   10
        For God doth know how many now in health
        Shall drop their blood in approbation
        Of what your reverence shall incite us to.
        Therefore take heed how you impawn our person,
        How you awake the sleeping sword of war: 15
        We charge you in the name of God take heed.
        After this conjuration, speak, my lord:
        And we will judge, note, and believe in heart
        That what you speak is washed as pure
        As sin in baptism.   20
BISHOP Then hear me, gracious sovereign, and you peers,
        Which owe your lives, your faith, and services
        To this imperial throne: there is no bar
        To stay your Highness' claim to France
        But one, which they produce from Pharamond: 25
        No female shall succeed in Salic land,
        Which Salic land the French unjustly glose

Scene 1 *Enter . . . Attendants* Q1; *Enter the King, Humfrey, Bedford, Clarence, Warwick, Westmerland, and Exeter.* F 1
th'ambassadors] Q1; th'Ambassador F 6 Sure] Q1 (Shure) 8 stop us] Q1; barre vs F 9 wise and learned] Q1; deare and
faithfull F 10 frame, or wrest] Q1; wrest, or bow F 10 same.] Q1; – , F 15 the] Q1; our F 17 After] Q1; Vnder F 18
judge] Q1; heare F 20 in] Q1; with F 21 you] Q1, F; yon Q3 22 lives, your faith] Q1; selues, your liues F 24 stay] Q1;
make against F 25 one] Q1; this F 26 female] Q1; Woman F

To be the realm of France, and Pharamond
The founder of this law and female bar.
Yet their own writers faithfully affirm   30
That the land Salic lies in Germany,
Between the floods of Sabeck and of Elbe,
Where Charles the Fifth, having subdued the Saxons,
There left behind and settled certain French,
Who, holding in disdain the German women   35
For some dishonest manners of their lives,
Established there this law. To wit,
No female shall succeed in Salic land;
Which Salic land, as I said before,
Is at this time in Germany called Meissen.   40
Thus doth it well appear the Salic law
Was not devisèd for the realm of France,
Nor did the French possess the Salic land
Until four hundred one-and-twenty years
After the function of King Pharamond,   45
Godly supposed the founder of this law.
Hugh Capet also, that usurped the crown,
To fine his title with some show of truth,
When in pure truth it was corrupt and naught,
Conveyed himself as heir to the Lady Inger,   50
Daughter to Charles, the foresaid Duke of Lorraine;
So that as clear as is the summer's sun,
King Pepin's title and Hugh Capet's claim,
King Charles his satisfaction, all appear
To hold in right and title of the female.   55
So do the lords of France until this day,
Howbeit they would hold up this Salic law
To bar your Highness claiming from the female,
And rather choose to hide them in a net
Than amply to embase their crooked causes,   60
Usurped from you and your progenitors.

KING May we with right and conscience make this claim?
BISHOP The sin upon my head, dread sovereign,
For in the Book of Numbers is it writ,
'When the son dies, let the inheritance   65

28 France,] F; − : Q1   30 writers] Q1; Authors F   31 lies] Q1; is F   33 Fifth] Q1; Great F   36 lives] Q1; life F   37 there]
Q1; then F   38 No . . . land] Q1; No Female / Should be Inheretrix in *Salike* Land F   39 as I said before] Q1; (as I haue
sayd before) Q3   40 time] Q1; day F   45 the function] Q1; defunction F   46 Godly] Q1; Idly F   48 fine] Q1; find F   48
show] Q1; shewes F   49 When] Q1; Though F   50 heir] Q1; th'Heire F   50 Inger] Q1; Lingare F   51 Charles . . . Lorraine]
Q1; *Charlemaine,* who was the Sonne / To F   54 Charles] Q1; *Lewes* F   56 lords] Q1; Kings F   56 until] Q1; vnto F   56
day,] Q1 − . F   57 Howbeit] Q1; − , F   60 embase] Q1 (imbace); embrace Q3; imbarre F   62 we] Q1; I F   64 is it] Q1, F; it
is Q3   65 son] Q1; man F

Descend unto the daughter'. Noble Lord,
Stand for your own, unwind your bloody flag,
Go, my dread Lord, to your great-grandsire's grave,
From whom you claim,
And your great-uncle Edward the Black Prince,   70
Who on the French ground played a tragedy,
Making defeat on the full power of France,
Whilst his most mighty father on a hill
Stood smiling to behold his lion's whelp
Foraging blood of French nobility.   75
O noble English, that could entertain
With half their forces the full power of France,
And let another half stand laughing by,
All out of work and cold for action.
KING We must not only arm us against the French,   80
But lay down our proportion for the Scot,
Who will make road upon us with all advantages.
BISHOP The marches, gracious sovereign, shall be sufficient
To guard your England from the pilfering borderers.
KING We do not mean the coursing sneakers only,   85
But fear the main intendment of the Scot.
For you shall read, never my great-grandfather
Unmasked his power for France
But that the Scot on his unfurnished kingdom
Came pouring like the tide into a breach,   90
That England, being empty of defences,
Hath shook and trembled at the bruit hereof.
BISHOP She hath been then more feared than hurt, my Lord.
For hear her but exemplified by herself,
When all her chivalry hath been in France,   95
And she a mourning widow of her nobles.
She hath herself not only well defended
But taken and impounded as a stray
The King of Scots,
Whom like a caitiff she did lead to France,   100
Filling your chronicles as rich with praise
As is the ooze and bottom of the sea
With sunken wreck and shipless treasury.

66 Noble] Q1; Gracious F   68 grave] Q1; Tombe F   70 uncle] Q1; Vnckles F   75 Foraging] Q1; Foraging the Q3; Forrage
in F   77 power] Q1; pride F   80 us against] Q1; t'inuade F   81 for] Q1; to defend / Against F   84 guard your] Q1; defend
our F   85 sneakers] Q1; snatchers F   88 Unmasked . . . for] Q1; went with his forces into F   91 defences] Q1; defence
F   92 bruit thereof] This edn; brute hereof Q1–3; th'ill neighbourhood F   93 hurt] Q1; harm'd F   93 Lord] Q1; liege F   94
exemplified] Q1; exampl'd F   100 like a caitiff] Q1; *not in* F   101 Filling . . . chronicles] Q1; And make their Chronicle F;
And make her Chronicle *Capell*; And make your Chronicle *Taylor*   103 wreck] Q1 (wrack); F   103 shipless treasury] Q1;
sum-lesse Treasuries F

LORD   There is a saying, very old and true,
        'If you will France win,   105
        Then with Scotland first begin'.
        For once the eagle England being in prey,
        To his unfurnished nest the weasel Scot
        Would suck her eggs, playing the mouse in absence of the cat,
        To spoil and havoc more than she can eat.   110
EXETER   It follows, then, the cat must stay at home.
        Yet that is but a cursed necessity,
        Since we have traps to catch the petty thieves.
        Whilst that the arméd hand doth fight abroad
        The adviséd head controls at home,   115
        For government though high or low, being put into parts,
        Congrueth with a mutual consent like music.
BISHOP   True; therefore doth heaven divide
        The fate of man in diverse functions.
        Whereto is added as an aim or butt, obedience;   120
        For so live the honey bees, creatures that by awe
        Ordain an act of order to a peopled kingdom.
        They have a king, and officers of sort,
        Where some like magistrates correct at home;
        Others like merchants venture trade abroad;   125
        Others like soldiers, arméd in their stings,
        Make boot upon the summer's velvet bud,
        Which pillage they with merry march bring home
        To the tent royal of their emperor,
        Who, busied in his majesty, behold   130
        The singing masons building roofs of gold,
        The civil citizens lading up the honey,
        The sad-eyed justice with his surly hum
        Delivering up to executors pale the lazy caning drone.
        This I infer, that twenty actions, once afoot,   135
        May all end in one moment.
        As many arrows, looséd several ways, fly to one mark,
        As many several ways meet in one town,
        As many fresh streams run in one self sea,
        As many lines close in the dial centre,   140

104 LORD] Q1; *Bish.Ely* F; *West. Capell*   **104** There is] Q1; But there's F   **105** If you] Q1; *If that you* F   **108** his] Q1; her F   **109** Would . . . eggs] Q1; Comes sneaking, and so sucks her Princely Egges F   **110** spoil] Q1; tame F   **112** cursed] Q1; crush'd F   **113** Since . . . traps] Q1; And pretty traps F   **115** controls] Q1; defends it selfe F   **116** being . . . parts] Q1; and lower, / Put into parts F   **116** into] Q1; in Q3   **117** mutual consent] Q1; full and natural close F   **118** True; therefore] Q1; Therefore F   **119** fate] Q1; state F   **120** added] Q1; fixed F   **121** live] Q1; worke F   **121** awe] Q1; a rule in Nature teach F   **123** sort] Q1; sorts F   **127** bud] Q1; buddes F   **130** behold] Q1; surueyes F   **132** lading] Q1; kneading F   **134** caning] Q1; yawning F   **135** twenty actions] Q1 (20. actions); many things F   **135** once afoot] Q1; hauing full reference / To one consent F   **136** end] Q1; And F   **136** end . . . moment] Q1; worke contrariously F   **137** fly] Q1; Come F   **138** several] Q1; *not in* F   **139** run] Q1; meet F   **139** self] Q1; salt F   **140** dial] Q1; Dials F

So may a thousand actions, once afoot,
End in one moment, and be all well borne
Without defect. Therefore, my Liege, to France.
Divide your happy England into four,
Of which take you one quarter into France,   145
And you withal shall make all Gallia shake.
If we, with thrice that power left at home,
Cannot defend our own door from the dog
Let us be beaten, and from henceforth lose
The name of policy and hardiness.   150
KING Call in the messenger sent from the Dauphin.
And by your aid, the noble sinews of our land,
France being ours, we'll bring it to our awe,
Or break it all in pieces. Either our chronicles
Shall with full mouth speak freely of our acts,   155
Or else like tongueless mutes
Not worshipped with a paper epitaph.

Enter the Ambassadors from France

Now are we well prepared to know the Dauphin's pleasure,
For we hear your coming is from him.
AMBASSADOR Pleaseth your Majesty to give us leave   160
Freely to render what we have in charge,
Or shall I sparingly show afar off
The Dauphin's pleasure and our embassage?
KING We are no tyrant, but a Christian king,
To whom our spirit is as subject   165
As are our wretches fettered in our prisons.
Therefore freely and with uncurbed boldness
Tell us the Dauphin's mind.
AMBASSADOR Then this in fine the Dauphin saith:
Whereas you claim certain towns in France   170
From your predecessor King Edward the Third,
This he returns: he saith there's nought in France
That can be with a nimble galliard won.
You cannot revel into dukedoms there.
Therefore he sendeth, meeter for your study,   175
This tun of treasure; and in lieu of this

142 moment] Q1; purpose F   143 defect] Q1; defeat F   145 Of which] Q1; Whereof, F   147 that power] Q1; such powers
F   148 door] Q1; doores F   149 beaten] Q1; worried F   149 from henceforth] Q1; our Nation F   150 policy and hardiness]
Q1; hardinesse and policie F   151 messenger] Q1; Messengers F   152 And . . . aid] Q1; and by Gods helpe / And yours,
F   152 land] Q1; power F   153 bring] Q1; bend F   154 chronicles] Q1; History F   157 paper] Q1; waxen F   159 from him]
Q1; from him, not from the King F   160 Pleaseth] Q1; May't please F   162 I] Q1; we F   162 afar] Q1; you farre F   165
To . . . spirit] Q1; Vnto whose grace our passion F   166 are] Q1; is F   167 boldness] Q1; plainnesse F   169 fine] Q1; few
F   175 sendeth] Q1; sends you F   175 study] Q1; spirit F

Desires to let the dukedoms that you crave
Hear no more from you. This the Dauphin saith.
KING What treasure, uncle?
EXETER   Tennis balls, my liege.
KING We are glad the Dauphin is so pleasant with us.   180
Your message and his present we accept.
When we have matched our rackets to these balls
We will by God's grace play such a set
Shall strike his father's crown into the hazard.
Tell him he hath made a match with such a wrangler   185
That all the courts of France shall be disturbed
With chases. And we understand him well,
How he comes o'er us with our wilder days,
Not measuring what use we made of them.
We never valued this poor seat of England,   190
And therefore gave our self to barbarous licence,
As 'tis common seen that men are merriest when they are from
     home
But tell the Dauphin we will keep our state,
Be like a king, mighty and command,
When we do rouse us in our throne of France.   195
For this have we laid by our majesty
And plodded like a man for working days.
But we will rise there with so full a glory
That we will dazzle all the eyes of France;
Aye, strike the Dauphin blind to look on us,   200
And tell him this, his mock hath turned his balls to gunstones
And his soul shall sit sore chargéd for the wasteful vengeance
That shall fly from them. For this his mock
Shall mock many a wife out of their dear husbands,
Mock mothers from their sons, mock castles down;   205
Aye, some are yet ungotten and unborn
That shall have cause to curse the Dauphin's scorn.
But this lies all within the will of God,
To whom we do appeal, and in whose name
Tell you the Dauphin we are coming on   210
To venge us as we may, and to put forth our hand

177 to let] Q1; you let F   177 crave] Q1; claime F   181 Your . . . present] Q1; His Present, and your paines F   181 accept] Q1; thanke you for F   183 play such a] Q1; play him such a Q3; play a F   183 will by] Q1; will in France by F   191 our self] F; our selues Q1–3   192 common seen] Q1; euer common F   193 we . . . our] Q1; I . . . my F   194 mighty and command] Q1; and shew my sayle of Greatnesse F   195 we . . . us] Q1; I . . . me F   195 our throne] *This edn*; throne Q1; the throne Q3; my Throne F   196 this have we . . . our] Q1; that I haue . . . my F   197 like] Q2, F; lide Q1   198 we] Q1; I F   198 with . . . a glory] F; with so full of glory Q1, Q3; so full of glory Q2   199 we] Q1; I F   200 Aye] Q1 (I); Yea F   201 him this] Q1; the pleasant Prince F   202 sit] Q1; stand F   203 from] Q1; with F   204 many a wife] Q1; many a thousand widows F   206 Aye,] Q1 (I); And F   209 we] Q1; I F   210 we are] Q1; I am F   211 us . . . we] Q1; me . . . I F

In a rightful cause. So get you hence, and tell your prince
His jest will savour but of shallow wit
When thousands weep more than did laugh at it.
Convey them with safe conduct. See them hence.   215
EXETER This was a merry message.
KING We hope to make the sender blush at it.
Therefore let our collection for the wars
Be soon provided, for, God before,
We'll check the Dauphin at his father's door.   220
Therefore let every man now task his thought,
That this fair action may on foot be brought.

Exeunt omnes

[2] *Enter* NIM *and* BARDOLPH

BARDOLPH Good morrow, Corporal Nim.
NIM Good morrow, Lieutenant Bardolph.
BARDOLPH What, is Ancient Pistol and thee friends yet?
NIM I cannot tell, things must be as they may. I dare not fight, but I will wink
and hold out mine iron. It is a simple one, but what though? It will serve to   5
toast cheese, and it will endure cold as another man's sword will, and
there's the humour of it.
BARDOLPH I'faith, Mistress Quickly did thee great wrong, for thou wert troth-
plight to her.
NIM I must do as I may. Though patience be a tired mare, yet she'll plod, and   10
some say knives have edges, and men may sleep and have their throats
about them at that time, and there is the humour of it.
BARDOLPH Come, i'faith, I'll bestow a breakfast to make Pistol and thee
friends. What a plague, should we carry knives to cut our own throats?
NIM I'faith, I'll live as long as I may, that's the certain of it. And when I cannot 15
live any longer, I'll do as I may, and there's my rest and the rendezvous of
it.

Enter PISTOL *and* HOSTESS QUICKLY, *his wife*

BARDOLPH Good morrow, Ancient Pistol. Here comes Ancient Pistol. I
prithee, Nym, be quiet.
NIM How do you, my host?   20
PISTOL Base slave, callest thou me host? Now by gad's lugs I swear, I scorn the
title, nor shall my Nell keep lodging.

212 rightful] Q1; right Q3   212 hence] Q1; hence in peace F   212 your prince] Q1; the *Dolphin* F   215 conduct] Q1; couduct
Q2   215 See them hence] Q1; Fare you well F   220 check the] Q1; chide this F   **Scene 2**   1 Good morrow Q1
(Godmorrow); Well met F   3 is] Q1; are F   7 the humour of it] Q1; an end F   8 Mistress Quickly] Q3; mistresse quickly
Q1–2   8 thou wert] Q1; you were F   10 mare] Q1; name F   16 my rest] Q1; the rest Q2   20 NIM] Q1; *not in* F   20
How . . . host] Q1; How now mine Hoaste *Pistoll* F   21 slave] Q1; Tyke F   21 gad's lugs] Q1; this hand F   22 lodging] Q1;
Lodgers F

HOSTESS No by my troth, not I, for we cannot bed nor board half a score honest
gentlewomen that live honestly by the prick of their needle but it is thought
straight we keep a bawdy house. O Lord, here's Corporal Nim, now shall   25
we have wilful adultery and murder committed! Good Corporal Nim, show
the valour of a man, and put up your sword.

NIM Push.

PISTOL What dost thou push, thou prick-eared cur of Iceland?

NIM Will you shog off? I would have you *solus*.   30

PISTOL Solus? Egregious dog, that solus in thy throat, and in thy lungs, and,
which is worse, within thy messful mouth! I do retort that solus in thy
bowels, and in thy jaw, perdie! For I can talk, and Pistol's flashing fiery
cock is up!

NIM I am not Barbason, you cannot conjure me. I have an humour, Pistol, to   35
knock you indifferently well. An you fall foul with me, Pistol, I'll scour you
with my rapier in fair terms. If you will walk off a little I'll prick your guts
a little in good terms, and there's the humour of it.

PISTOL O braggart vile, and damnéd furious wight! The grave doth gape, and
groaning Death is near, therefore exhale!   40

They draw

BARDOLPH Hear me! He that strikes the first blow, I'll kill him, as I am a
soldier.

PISTOL An oath of mickle might, and fury shall abate.

NIM I'll cut your throat at one time or another in fair terms, and there's the
humour of it.   45

PISTOL 'Couple gorge' is the word, I thee defy again. A damnéd hound, thinkst
thou my spouse to get? No, to the powdering tub of infamy! Fetch forth the
lazar kite of Cressid's kind, Doll Tearsheet, she by name, and her espouse!
I have, and I will hold, the quondam Quickly, for the only she, and *Paco*!
There it is enough.   50

Enter the BOY

BOY Hostess, you must come straight to my master, and you, Host Pistol. Good
Bardolph, put thy nose between the sheets, and do the office of a warming
pan.

HOSTESS By my troth he'll yield the crow a pudding one of these days. I'll go
to him. Husband, you'll come?   55

BARDOLPH Come, Pistol, be friends. Nim, prithee be friends, and if thou wilt
not, be enemies with me too.

23 half a score] Q1; a dozen or foureteene F   23 honest] Q1; *not in* Q3   25 Nim] Q2, Q3, F; *Nims.* Q1   27 the valour . . . man]
Q1; thy valor F   28 Push] Q1; Pish F   32 messful] nastie F   32 talk] Q1; take F   35 Barbason] F; *Barbasom* Q1–3   40
groaning] Q1; doting F   40 exhale] F; exall Q1   41 blow] Q1; stroke F   41 kill him] Q1; run him vp to the hilts F   44 your]
Q1; thy F   44 fair] Q1; good F   46 thee defy] Q1; defie thee F   46 A damnéd hound] Q1 O hound of Creet F   49 quondam
Quickly] F; quandom quickly Q1–3   49 *Paco!*] Q1 *Pauca* F   50 enough] Q1; enough to go to F   51 Hostess] Q1; Mine Hoast
Pistoll F   51 you, Host Pistol] Q1; your Hostess F   52 nose] Q1; face F   52 the] Q1; his F   54 days] Q1; dayes: the King
has kild his heart F

NIM I shall have my eight shillings I won of you at betting?
PISTOL Base is the slave that pays.
NIM That now I will have, and there's the humour of it.   60
PISTOL As manhood shall compound.

They draw

BARDOLPH He that strikes the first blow, I'll kill him by this sword.
PISTOL 'Sword' is an oath, and oaths must have their course.
NIM I shall have my eight shillings I won of you at betting?
PISTOL A noble shalt thou have, and ready pay, and liquor likewise will I give   65
to thee, and friendship shall combine, and brotherhood! I'll live by Nim as
Nim shall live by me. Is not this just? For I shall sutler be unto the camp,
and profit will accrue.
NIM I shall have my noble?
PISTOL In cash most truly paid.   70
NIM Why, there's the humour of it.

Enter HOSTESS

HOSTESS As ever you came of men, come in! Sir John, poor soul, is so troubled
with a burning tertian contagian fever, 'tis wonderful.
PISTOL Let us condole the knight, for, lambkins, we will live!

Exeunt omnes

[3] *Enter* EXETER *and* GLOSTER

GLOSTER Before God, my Lord, his Grace is too bold to trust these traitors.
EXETER They shall be apprehended by and by.
GLOSTER Aye, but the man that was his bedfellow,
Whom he hath cloyed and graced with princely favours,
That he should for a foreign purse to sell   5
His sovereign's life to death and treachery!
EXETER Oh, the Lord of Masham.

Enter the KING *and three lords*

KING Now sirs, the wind's fair, and we will aboard.
My Lord of Cambridge, and my Lord of Masham,
And you my gentle knight, give me your thoughts.   10

58 I shall have] Q1; You'l pay me F   58 betting] Q3; beating Q1   58] NIM. I . . . betting (beating) Q1; *not in* F   65 ready] Q1; present F   66 combine, and] F; combind and Q1; combinde out Q3   66 as] Q1; and F   67 sutler] Q1; Butler Q2   68 profit] Q1; profits F   68 accrue] F; occrue Q1–3   70 truly] Q1; iustly F   72 came of men] Q1; come of women F   73 tertian contagian] Q1 (contigian); quotidian Tertain F   Scene 3   1 my Lord] Q1; *not in* F   1 too bold] Q1; bold F   4 cloyed and graced] Q1; dull'd and cloy'd F   4 favours] Q1; fauour: Q2   5 to sell] Q1; so sell F   7 Oh . . . Masham] Q1; *not in* F   8 sirs] Q1; sits F   8 wind's] Q1 (windes); winde is Q3; winde F   9 Lord of] Q1; kinde lord F

Do you not think the power we bear with us
Will make us conquerors in the field of France?
MASHAM No doubt, my Liege, if each man do his best.
CAMBRIDGE Never was monarch better feared and loved than is your Majesty.
GRAY Even those that were your father's enemies   15
    Have steeped their galls in honey for your sake.
KING We therefore have great cause of thankfulness,
    And shall forget the office of our hands
    Sooner than reward and merit
    According to their cause and worthiness.   20
MASHAM So service shall with steeléd sinews shine,
    And labour shall refresh itself with hope
    To do your Grace incessant service.
KING Uncle of Exeter, enlarge the man
    Committed yesterday, that railed against our person.   25
    We consider it was the heat of wine that set him on,
    And on his more advice we pardon him.
MASHAM That is mercy, but too much security.
    Let him be punished, sovereign, lest the example of him
    Breed more of such a kind.   30
KING O let us yet be merciful.
CAMBRIDGE So may your Highness, and punish too.
GRAY You show great mercy if you give him life
    After the taste of his correction.
KING Alas, your too much care and love of me   35
    Are heavy orisons 'gainst the poor wretch.
    If little faults proceeding on distemper
    Should not be winked at, how should we stretch our eye
    When capital crimes, chewed, swallowed, and digested,
    Appear before us? We'll yet enlarge the man,   40
    Though Cambridge and the rest in their dear loves
    And tender preservation of our state
    Would have him punished. Now to our French causes.
    Who are the late commissioners?
CAMBRIDGE   Me one, my Lord,
    Your highness bade me ask for it today.   45
MASHAM So did you me, my Sovereign.
GRAY   And me, my Lord.

11 power] Q1; powres F   12 make . . . field] Q1; cut their passage through the force F   13 MASHAM] Q1; *Scro.* F   15 Even those] Q1; True: those F   18 hands] Q1; hand F   19 Sooner . . . merit] Q1; *not in* Q3   19 reward] Q1; quittance of desert F   20 their cause] Q1; the weight F   21 shine] Q1; toyle F   23 service] Q1; seruices F   24 Uncle] Q1; We Iudge no less. Vnkle F   26 the heat] Q1; excesse F   28 That is] Q1; That's F   29 the . . . him] Q1; example F   30 Breed] Q1; Breed (by his sufferance) F   32 and] Q1; and yet F   33 You] Q1; Sir, you F   34 his] Q1; much F   35 care and love] Q1; loue and care F   38 should] Q1; shall F   38 Should . . . should] Q1; Shall . . . shall F   40 Appear] Q1; Appeared Q2   40 the] Q1; that F   41 and the rest] Q1; *Scroope, and Gray* F   41 loves] Q1; care F   42 state] Q1; person F   44 Me] Q1; I F   46 Sovereign] Q1; Liege F

KING Then, Richard, Earl of Cambridge, there is yours.
　　　　There is yours, my Lord of Masham,
　　　　And Sir Thomas Gray, Knight of Northumberland, this same is
　　　　　yours.
　　　　Read them, and know we know your worthiness.   50
　　　　Uncle Exeter, I will aboard tonight.
　　　　Why how now, gentlemen, why change you colour?
　　　　What see you in those papers
　　　　That hath so chased your blood out of appearance?
CAMBRIDGE I do confess my fault, and do submit me   55
　　　　To your Highness' mercy.
MASHAM   To which we all appeal.
KING The mercy which was quick in us but late
　　　　By your own reasons is forestalled and done.
　　　　You must not dare for shame to ask for mercy,
　　　　For your own conscience turn upon your bosoms,   60
　　　　As dogs upon their masters, worrying them.
　　　　See you my princes, and my noble peers,
　　　　These English monsters: my Lord of Cambridge here,
　　　　You know how apt we were to grace him
　　　　In all things belonging to his honour.   65
　　　　And this vile man hath for a few light crowns
　　　　Lightly conspired and sworn unto the practices of France
　　　　To kill us here in Hampton. To the which
　　　　This knight, no less in bounty bound to us
　　　　Than Cambridge is, hath likewise sworn.   70
　　　　But oh, what shall I say to thee, false man,
　　　　Thou cruel, ungrateful and inhuman creature,
　　　　Thou that didst bear the key of all my counsel,
　　　　That knew'st the very secrets of my heart,
　　　　That almost might'st ha' coined me into gold,   75
　　　　Would'st thou ha' practised on me for thy use?
　　　　Can it be possible that out of thee
　　　　Should proceed one spark that might annoy my finger?
　　　　'Tis so strange, that though the truth doth show as gross
　　　　As black from white, mine eye will scarcely see it.   80
　　　　Their faults are open, arrest them to the answer of the law,
　　　　And God acquit them of their practices.

48 my Lord] Q1; Lord *Scroope* F 49 Thomas . . . Knight] Q1; Knight, / *Gray* F 50 we] Q1; I F 51 Uncle Exeter] Q1; My lord of *Westmerland*, and Vnkle *Exeter* F 51 I] Q1; We F 54 hath] Q1; haue F 54 chased] Q1; cowarded and chac'd F 57 quick] F; quit Q1 58 reasons] Q1; counsaile F 58 forestalled and done] Q1; supprest and kill'd F 59 ask for] Q1; talke of F 60 conscience] Q1; reasons F 60 upon] Q1; into F 61 them] Q1; you F 64–5 we . . . things] Q1 our loue was, to accord / To furnish with all appertinents F 66 vile] Q2; Q1, Q3 vilde; *not in* F 69 in] Q1; for F 70 hath] Q2; haah Q1 71 false man] Q1; Lord *Scroope* F 72 and inhuman] Q1; sauage, and inhumane F 73 counsel] Q1; counsailes F 74 secrets . . . heart] Q1 bottome of my soule F 75 ha' coined] Q1 (a coyned); haue coined F 76 ha' practised] Q1 (a practisde); haue practis'd F 79 truth doth show] Q1; truth of it stands off F 80 from] Q1; and F; on *Maxwell*

EXETER I arrest thee of high treason, by the name of Richard, Earl of Cam-
bridge. I arrest thee of high treason, by the name of Henry, Lord of
Masham. I arrest thee of high treason, by the name of Thomas Gray,   85
Knight of Northumberland.

MASHAM Our purposes God justly hath discovered,
    And I repent my fault more than my death,
    Which I beseech your Majesty forgive,
    Although my body pay the price of it.   90

KING God quit you in His mercy. Hear your sentence.
    You have conspired against our royal person,
    Joined with an enemy proclaimed and fixed,
    And from his coffers received the golden earnest of our death.
    Touching our person, we seek no redress.   95
    But we our kingdom's safety must so tender
    Whose ruin you have sought, that to our laws
    We do deliver you. Get ye therefore hence,
    Poor miserable creatures, to your death,
    The taste whereof God in His mercy give   100
    You patience to endure, and true repentance
    Of all your deeds amiss. Bear them hence.

                                     Exit three lords

    Now lords, to France, the enterprise whereof
    Shall be to you as us, successively.
    Since God cut off this dangerous treason lurking in our way,   105
    Cheerily to sea. The signs of war advance.
    No King of England if not King of France!

                                       Exit omnes

[4] *Enter* NIM, PISTOL, BARDOLPH, HOSTESS, *and a* BOY

HOSTESS I prithee, sweetheart, let me bring thee so far as Staines.
PISTOL No fur, no fur.
BARDOLPH Well, Sir John is gone, God be with him.
HOSTESS Aye, he is in Arthur's bosom, if ever any were. He went away as if it
were a Christomed child, between twelve and one, just at turning of the   5
tide. His nose was as sharp as a pen; for when I saw him fumble with the
sheets and talk of flowers and smile upon his fingers' ends I knew there was

84–5 Henry . . . Masham] Q1; *Thomas* Lord *Scroope* of Masham F   89 Majesty forgive] Q1; Highnesse to forgiue F   93 and fixed] Q1; *not in* F   95 we . . . redress] Q1; seeke we no reuenge F   97 have] Q1; *not in* F   98 ye] Q1; you F   102 deeds amiss] Q1; deare offences F   103 to] Q1; for F   104 successively] Q1; like glorious F   **Scene 4**   1 sweetheart] Q1; honey sweet Husband F   1 so far as] Q1; to F   3 Sir John] Q1; *Falstaffe* F   5 just] Q1; eu'n F   7 talk of flowers] Q1; a Table of greene fields F; a babbled of green fields Theobald

no way but one. How now, Sir John? quoth I, and he cried three times God, God, God! Now I, to comfort him, bade him not think of God, I hope there was no such need. Then he bade me put more clothes at his feet. And I felt   10
to them, and they were as cold as any stone; and to his knees, and they were as cold as any stone; and so upward, and upward, and all was as cold as any stone.

NIM They say he cried out on sack.

HOSTESS Aye, that he did.   15

BOY And of women.

HOSTESS No, that he did not.

BOY Yea, that he did, and he said they were devils incarnate.

HOSTESS Indeed, carnation was a colour he never loved.

NIM Well, he did cry out on women.   20

HOSTESS Indeed he did in some sort handle women, but then he was rheumatic, and talked of the Whore of Babylon.

BOY Hostess, do you remember he saw a flea stand upon Bardolph's nose, and said it was a black soul burning in hell fire?

BARDOLPH Well, God be with him, that was all the wealth I got in his service.   25

NIM Shall we shog off? The King will be gone from Southampton.

PISTOL Clear up thy crystals, look to my chattels and my moveables. Trust none: the word is pitch and pay. Men's words are wafer cakes, and Holdfast is the only dog, my dear. Therefore Cophetua be thy counsellor. Touch her soft lips and part.   30

BARDOLPH Farewell, Hostess.

NIM I cannot kiss, and there's the humour of it. But adieu.

PISTOL Keep fast thy bugle bow.

Exit omnes

[5] *Enter King of* FRANCE, BOURBON, DAUPHIN, [CONSTABLE], *and others*

FRENCH KING Now you Lords of Orleans, of Bourbon and of Berry,
              You see the King of England is not slack,
              For he is footed on this land already.

DAUPHIN My gracious Lord, 'tis meet we all go forth,
              And arm us against the foe,   5
              And view the weak and sickly parts of France.
              But let us do it with no show of fear,
              No, with no more than if we heard

10 put] Q1; lay F   10 at] Q1; on Q3   12 as any] Q1; as Q3   14 on] Q1; of F   15 he] Q1; a F   18 Yea] Q1; Yes Q3   18 incarnate] Q1 (incarnat); incarnste Q3   19 loved] Q1; lik'd F   23 stand] Q1; strike F   24 hell fire] Q1; hell Q3, F   25 God . . . him] Q1; the fuel is gone that maintain'd that fire F   25 wealth] Q1; riches F   26 shog off] Q1; shogg F   28 word] Q1; world Q2, F   29 dear] Q1; Ducke F   29 Cophetua] Q1; *caueto* F   **Scene 5**   4 gracious Lord] Q1; most redoubted Father F   6 weak and sickly] Q1; sick and feeble F   7 But] Q1; And F

England were busied with a morris dance.
For, my good Lord, she is so idly kinged,   10
Her sceptre so fantastically borne,
So guided by a shallow humorous youth,
That fear attends her not.
CONSTABLE O peace, prince Dauphin, you deceive yourself.
Question, your Grace, the late ambassador,   15
With what regard he heard his embassage,
How well supplied with agéd counsellors,
And how his resolution answered him.
You then would say that Harry was not wild.
FRENCH KING Well, think we Harry strong,   20
And strongly arm us to prevent the foe.
CONSTABLE My Lord, here is an ambassador
From the King of England.
FRENCH KING   Bid him come in.
You see this chase is hotly followed, lords.
DAUPHIN My gracious father, cut up this English short.   25
Self-love, my Liege, is not so vile a thing
As self-neglecting.

Enter EXETER

FRENCH KING   From our brother England?
EXETER From him, and thus he greets your Majesty.
He wills you, in the name of God almighty,
That you divest yourself and lay apart   30
That borrowed title, which by gift of heaven,
Of law of nature, and of nations, 'longs
To him and to his heirs, namely, the crown,
And all wide-stretchéd titles that belongs
Unto the crown of France. That you may know   35
'Tis no sinister, nor no awkward claim,
Picked from the worm-holes of old vanished days,
Nor from the dust of old oblivion rack't,
He sends you these most memorable lines,
In every branch truly demonstrated;   40
Willing you overlook this pedigree,
And when you find him evenly derived
From his most famed and famous ancestors,

9 busied] Q1; troubled Q3   9 morris dance] Q1; Whitson Morris-dance F   12 So guided by a] Q1; By a vaine giddie F   14 you deceive yourself] Q1; You are too much mistaken in this King F   15 ambassador] Q1; Embassadors F   16 regard] Q1; great State F   17 aged] Q1; Noble F   20 Well . . . Harry] Q1; Thinke we King Harry F   23 Bid . . . in] Q1 Goe, and bring them F   24 lords] Q1; friends F   25 cut . . . short] Q1; Take vp the English short F   26 thing] Q1; sinne F   27 brother] Q1; brother of Q3   31 title] Q1; Glories F   34 titles] Q1; Honors F   34 belongs] Q1; pertain F   37 old] Q1; long F   39 these . . . lines] Q1; this . . . Lyne F   40 demonstrated] Q1; demonstratiue F   43 and] Q1; of F

Edward the Third, he bids you then resign
Your crown and kingdom, indirectly held   45
From him, the native and true challenger.
FRENCH KING If not, what follows?
EXETER Bloody constraint, for if you hide the crown
Even in your hearts, there will he rake for it.
Therefore in fierce tempest is he coming,   50
In thunder and in earthquake, like a Jove,
That if requiring fail, he will compel it.
And on your heads turns he the widow's tears,
The orphan's cries, the dead men's bones,
The pining maiden's groans,   55
For husbands, fathers, and distressèd lovers,
Which shall be swallowed in this controversy.
This is his claim, his threatening, and my message,
Unless the Dauphin be in presence here,
To whom expressly we bring greeting too.   60
DAUPHIN For the Dauphin? I stand here for him.
What to hear from England?
EXETER Scorn and defiance, slight regard, contempt,
And anything that may not misbecome
The mighty sender, doth he prize you at.   65
Thus saith my King. Unless your father's Highness
Sweeten the bitter mock you sent his Majesty,
He'll call you to so loud an answer for it,
That caves and wombly vaults of France
Shall chide your trespass, and return your mock,   70
In second accent of his ordinance.
DAUPHIN Say that my father render fair reply,
It is against my will, for I desire
Nothing so much as odds with England,
And for that cause according to his youth   75
I did present him with those Paris balls.
EXETER He'll make your Paris Louvre shake for it,
Were it the mistress court of mighty Europe,
And be assured, you'll find a difference
As we his subjects have in wonder found,   80
Between his younger days and these he musters now;
Now he weighs time even to the latest grain,

47 If not] Q1; Or else F 52 compel it] Q1; compel F 53 turns he] Q1; Turning F 54 bones] Q1; Blood F 55 pining] Q1;
priuy F; privéd *Walter* 56 distressed] Q1; betrothed F 57 Which] Q1; That F 58 his claim] Q1; the claime Q2 60 we]
Q1; I F 62 hear] Q1; him F 66 Unless] Q1; and if F 68 loud] Q1; hot F 68 for] Q1; of F 69 wombly] Q1; Wombie F 72
that] Q1; if F 72 reply] Q1; returne F 74 so much as] Q1; but F 75 And . . . according] Q1; To that end, as matching
F 76 those] Q1; the F 81 his . . . musters] Q1; the promise of his greener dayese, / And these he masters F 82 latest] Q1,
vtmost F

Which you shall find in your own losses
If he stay in France.
FRENCH KING Well, for us, you shall return our answer back   85
To our brother England.

Exit omnes

[6] *Enter* NIM, BARDOLPH, PISTOL, BOY

NIM Before God, here is hot service.
PISTOL 'Tis hot indeed.
Blows go and come, God's vassals drop and die.
NIM 'Tis honour, and there's the humour of it.
BOY Would I were in London. I'd give all my honour for a pot of ale.   5
PISTOL And I. If wishes would prevail,
I would not stay, but thither would I hie.

Enter LLEWELLYN, *and beats them in*

LLEWELLYN God's plut, up to the breaches, you rascals, will you not up to the
breaches?
NIM Abate thy rage, sweet knight, abate thy rage!   10
BOY Well, I would I were once from them. They would have me as familiar
with men's pockets as their gloves and their handkerchiefs. They will steal
anything. Bardolph stole a lute case, carried it three mile, and sold it for
three ha'pence. Nim stole a fire shovel. I knew by that they meant to carry
coals. Well, if they will not leave me, I mean to leave them.   15

Exit NIM, BARDOLPH, PISTOL, *and the* BOY

Enter GOWER

GOWER Captain Llewellyn, you must come straight to the mines, to the Duke
of Gloucester.
LLEWELLYN Look you, tell the Duke it is not so good to come to the mines.
The concavities is otherwise. You may discuss to the Duke, the enemy is
digged himself five yards under the countermines. By Jesus, I think he'll   20
blow up all if there be no better direction.

Enter the KING *and his lords. Alarum*

KING How yet resolves the Governor of the town?
This is the latest parley we'll admit,

83 find] Q1; reade F   86 brother] Q1; brother of Q3   **Scene 6   1** here is] Q1; heres Q3   **3** Blows] Q1; Knocks F   **7**
I . . . stay] Q1; with me, my purpose shall not fayle with me F   **8** God's plut] Q1; *not in* F   **10** sweet knight] Q1; Great Duke
F   **13** three mile] Q1; twelue Leagues F   **16** straight] Q1; presently F   **19** enemy] Q1; athuersarie F   **20** Jesus] Q1; Ieshu
Q3   **21** no . . . direction] Q1; not better directions F   **21.1** *Enter . . . Alarum.*] Q1; *Alarum. Enter . . .* Q3   **23** parley we'll]
Q1; Parle we will F

Therefore to our best mercy give yourselves,
Or like to men proud of destruction,   25
Defy us to our worst. For as I am a soldier,
A name that in my thoughts becomes me best,
If we begin the battery once again
I will not leave the half-achieved Harfleur
Till in her ashes she be buriéd.   30
The gates of mercy are all shut up.
What say you, will you yield and this avoid,
Or, guilty in defence, be thus destroyed?

                    Enter GOVERNOR

GOVERNOR Our expectation hath this day an end.
    The Dauphin, whom of succour we entreated,   35
    Returns us word his powers are not yet ready
    To raise so great a siege. Therefore, dread King,
    We yield our town and lives to thy soft mercy.
    Enter our gates, dispose of us and ours,
    For we no longer are defensive now.   40
                                               [Exeunt]

[7] *Enter* KATHERINE, ALICE

KATE *Alice, venez ici. Vous avez quatorze ans, vous parlez fort bon anglais
    d'Angleterre. Comment s'appelez-vous la main en anglais?*
ALICE *La main, madame?* De han.
KATE *Et la bras?*
ALICE De arma, *madame.*   5
KATE *La main,* de hand; *le bras,* de arma.
ALICE *Ah, oui, madame.*
KATE *Et comment s'appelez-vous le menton et le col?*
ALICE De neck, *et* de cin, *madame.*
KATE De neck, *et* de cin. *Et le coude?*   10
ALICE *Le coude, ma foi, j'ai oublié, mais je remembre, le coude, oh,* de elbow,
    madame.
KATE *Ecoutez, je raconte tout celle que j'ai apprendré:* de han, de arma, de neck,
    de sin, *et* de bilbow.
ALICE De elbow, *madame.*   15

28 we] Q1; I F   30 be] Q1; lye F   31 are] Q1; shall be F   35 succour] Q1; succout Q3; succours F   36 word] Q1; that F   36
not yet] Q1; yet not F   37 dread] Q1; great F   40 defensive now] Q1; defensible F   **Scene 7**   1 *quatorze ans*] Q; *tu as este
en Angleterre* F   2 *Comment s'appelez-vous*] Q (Coman sae palla vou); *Comient appelle vous* F; francoy Q1–3   9
cin] Q1; sin Q3   10 cin] Q1; sin Q3   11 *le coude*] le tude Q1–Q3; *le coudre* F   13 *raconte*] This edn; recontera Q1   14 cin]
Q1; sin Q3

KATE *Oh Jesu, j'ai oublié. Ma foi, écoutez, je raconterai:* de han, de arma, de neck,
de cin, *et* de elbow. *Eh, c'est bon!*

ALICE *Ma foi, madame, vous parlez aussi bon anglais comme si vous avez été en
Angleterre.*

KATE *Par la grace de Dieu, en petit temps je parle meilleur. Comment s'appelez-vous* 20
le pied et le robe?

ALICE Le foot, *et* le con.

KATE Le fot, *et* le con. *Oh Jesu! Je ne veux point parler, si plus devant les chères
chevaliers de France, pour un million, ma foi!*

ALICE *Madame,* de foot, *et* le con.   25

KATE *Oh, est-il avisé? Ecoutez, Alice,* de han, de arma, de neck, de cin, le foot,
et le con.

ALICE *C'est fort bon, madame.*

KATE *Allons a dîner.*

                                                           Exit omnes

[8] *Enter King of* FRANCE, *Lord* CONSTABLE, *the* DAUPHIN, *and* BOURBON

FRENCH KING 'Tis certain he is past the river Somme.

CONSTABLE *Mortdieu, ma vie,* shall a few sprays of us,
              The emptying of our fathers' luxury,
              Outgrow their grafters?

BOURBON Normans, bastard Normans, *mortdieu!*   5
              An if they pass unfought withal,
              I'll sell my dukedom for a foggy farm
              In that short nook isle of England.

CONSTABLE Why, whence have they this mettle?
              Is not their climate raw, foggy, and cold,   10
              On whom as in disdain the sun looks pale?
              Can barley broth, a drench for swollen jades,
              Their sodden water, decoct such lively blood?
              And shall our quick blood, spirited with wine,
              Seem frosty? Oh, for honour of our names   15
              Let us not hang like frozen icicles
              Upon our houses' tops, while they, a more frosty climate,
              Sweat drops of youthful blood.

FRENCH KING Constable, dispatch, send Montjoy forth,
              To know what willing ransom he will give.   20
              Son Dauphin, you shall stay in Rouen with me.

17 cin] Q1; sin Q3   23 fot] Q1; foot Q3, F   26 cin] Q1; sin Q3   29 *Allons*] Q1 (*Aloues*); *alons nous* F   **Scene 8**   1 is] Q1; hath
F   2 sprays] F (Sprayes); spranes Q1   4 Outgrow] Q1; ouer-looke F   6 pass] Q1; march along F   7 for a foggy] Q1; To buy
a slobbry and a durty F   8 short nook] Q1; nook-shotten F   8 England] Q1; Albion F   9 Why] Q1; *Dieu de Battailes* F   10
cold] Q1; dull F   11 disdain] Q1; despight F   12 swollen] Q1; sur-reyned F   16 frozen] Q1; roping F   17 houses' tops] Q1
(houses); houses tops Q2, Q3; houses Thatch F

DAUPHIN Not so, I do beseech your Majesty.
FRENCH KING Well, I say it shall be so.

Exeunt omnes

[9] *Enter* GOWER [*and* LLEWELLYN]

GOWER How now, Captain Llewellyn, come you from the bridge?
LLEWELLYN By Jesus, there's excellent service committed at the bridge.
GOWER Is the Duke of Exeter safe?
LLEWELLYN The Duke of Exeter is a man whom I love, and I honour, and
    I worship with my soul, and my heart, and my life, and my lands and my   5
    livings, and my uttermost powers. The Duke is, look you, God be praised
    and pleased for it, no harm in the worell. He is maintain the bridge very
    gallantly. There is an ensign there, I do not know how you call him, but by
    Jesus I think he is as valiant a man as Mark Antony. He doth maintain the
    bridge most gallantly, yet he is a man of no reckoning. But I did see him do   10
    gallant service.
GOWER How do you call him?
LLEWELLYN His name is Ancient Pistol.
GOWER I know him not.

Enter Ancient PISTOL

LLEWELLYN Do you not know him? Here comes the man.   15
PISTOL Captain, I thee beseech to do me favour. The Duke of Exeter doth love
    thee well.
LLEWELLYN Aye, and I praise God I have merited some love at his hands.
PISTOL Bardolph, a soldier, one of buxom valour, hath by furious fate and
    giddy Fortune's fickle wheel, that goddess blind that stands upon the   20
    rolling restless stone –
LLEWELLYN By your patience, Ancient Pistol, Fortune, look you, is painted
    plind, with a muffler before her eyes, to signify to you that Fortune is
    plind. And she is moreover painted with a wheel, which is the moral that
    Fortune is turning, and inconstant, and variation, and mutabilities, and her   25
    fate is fixed at a spherical stone, which rolls and rolls and rolls. Surely the
    poet is make an excellent description of Fortune. Fortune, look you, is an
    excellent moral.
PISTOL Fortune is Bardolph's foe, and frowns on him, for he hath stolen a pax,
    and hangéd must he be. A damnéd death, let gallows gape for dogs, let man   30

Scene 9   2 service] Q1; Seruices F   7 is maintain] Q1; keepes F   8 ensign] Q1; aunchient Lieutenant F   9 Jesus] Q1; Ieshu
Q3   9 valiant a man as] Q1; valiant as Q3   10 reckoning] Q1; estimation in the World F   12 How] Q1; What F   13
His . . . is] Q1; Hee is call'd F   16 me] Q1; me a Q3   16 favour] Q1; fauours F   19 one of] Q1; and of F   20 goddess] Q1
(Godes); God's Q3   22 look you] Q1; *not in* F   23 her] Q1; his F   24 is moreover painted] Q1; is painted also F   24 that]
Q1; of it, that F   25 Fortune] Q1; shee F   25 variation, and mutabilities] Q1; mutabilitie, and variation F   26 fate] Q1; foot,
looke you F   27 is make] Q1; makes F   30 he] Q1; a F   30 dogs] Q1; Dogge F

go free, and let not death his windpipe stop. But Exeter hath given the
doom of death, for pax of petty price. Therefore go speak, the Duke will
hear thy voice, and let not Bardolph's vital thread be cut, with edge of
penny cord, and vile approach. Speak, captain, for his life, and I will thee
requite.   35

LLEWELLYN Captain Pistol, I partly understand your meaning.

PISTOL Why then, rejoice therefore.

LLEWELLYN Certainly, Ancient Pistol, 'tis not a thing to rejoice at, for if he
were my own brother, I would wish the Duke to do his pleasure, and put
him to executions, for look you, disciplines ought to be kept, they ought to   40
be kept.

PISTOL Die and be damned, and *figa* for thy friendship.

LLEWELLYN That is good.

PISTOL The fig of Spain within thy jaw.

LLEWELLYN That is very well.   45

PISTOL I say the fig within thy bowels and thy dirty maw.

Exit PISTOL

LLEWELLYN Captain Gower, cannot you hear it lighten and thunder?

GOWER Why, is this the Ancient you told me of? I remember him now, he is a
bawd, a cutpurse.

LLEWELLYN By Jesus, he is utter as prave words upon the bridge as you shall   50
desire to see in a summer's day. But it's all one, what he hath said to me,
look you, is all one.

GOWER Why, this is a gull, a fool, a rogue that goes to the wars only to grace
himself at his return to London. And such fellows as he are perfect in great
commanders' names. They will learn by rote where services were done, at   55
such and such a scene, at such a breach, at such a convoy, who came off
bravely, who was shot, who disgraced, what terms the enemy stood on.
And this they con perfectly in phrase of war, which they trick up with new
tuned oaths, and what a beard of the General's cut and a horrid shout of the
camp will do among the foaming bottles and ale-washed wits is wonderful   60
to be thought on. But you must learn to know such slanders of this age, or
else you may marvellously be mistook.

LLEWELLYN Certain, Captain Gower, it is not the man, look you, that I did
take him to be, but when time shall serve I shall tell him a little of my
desires. Here comes his Majesty.   65

Enter KING, CLARENCE, GLOSTER, *and others*

31 death] Q1; Hempe F   31 stop] Q1; suffocate F   32 petty] Q1; little F   34 approach] Q1; reproach F   36 Captain] Q1;
Aunchient F   39 my own] Q1; my F   39 wish] Q1; desire F   40 disciplines] Q1; discipline F   40 kept] Q1; vsed F   40–1
they . . . kept] Q1; *not in* F   42 *figa*] Q1; a fig Q3 *figo* F   42 That . . . good] Q1 It is well F   44 within . . . jaw] Q1; *not in*
F   46 I say . . . maw] Q1; *not in* F   47 LLEWELLYN . . . thunder?] Q1; *not in* F   48 is . . . is] Q1; this is an arrant counterfeit
Rascall, I remember him now: F   50 he is utter] Q1; a vtt'red F   51 it's all one] Q1; it is very well F   51 said] Q1; spoke
F   54 as he] Q1; *not in* F   54 great] Q1; the great F   56 scene] Q1; Sconce Q3, F   58 con] Q1; can Q2   59 shout] Q1; Sute
F   62 marvellously be] Q1; be marvellously F   64–5 a little . . . desires] Q1; my minde F

KING How now, Llewellyn, come you from the bridge?

LLEWELLYN Aye, an it shall please your Majesty, there is excellent service at the bridge.

KING What men have you lost, Llewellyn?

LLEWELLYN An it shall please your Majesty, the partition of the adversary 70
hath been great, very reasonably great, but for our own parts, like you now,
I think we have lost never a man, unless it be one for robbing of a church,
one Bardolph, if your Majesty know the man. His face is full of whelks and
knobs and pimples, and his breath blows at his nose like a coal, sometimes
red, sometimes plue. But God be praised, now his nose is executed, and his 75
fire out.

KING We would have all offenders so cut off, and we here give express com-
mandment that there be nothing taken from the villages but paid for, none
of the French abused or upbraided with disdainful language, for when
cruelty and lenity play for a kingdom the gentlest gamester is the sooner 80
winner.

Enter French HERALD

HERALD You know me by my habit.

KING Well then, we know thee. What should we know of thee?

HERALD My master's mind.

KING Unfold it.   85

HERALD Go thee unto Harry of England, and tell him, advantage is a better
soldier than rashness. Although we did seem dead, we did but slumber.
Now we speak upon our cue, and our voice is imperial. England shall
repent her folly, see her rashness, and admire our sufferance, which to
ransom, his pettiness would bow under. For the effusion of our blood, his 90
army is too weak. For the disgrace we have borne, himself kneeling at our
feet a weak and worthless satisfaction. To this, add defiance. So much from
the King my master.

KING What is thy name? We know thy quality.

HERALD Montjoy.   95

KING Thou dost thy office fair. Return thee back,
      And tell thy King I do not seek him now,
      But could be well content, without impeach,
      To march on to Calais. For to say the sooth,
      Though 'tis no wisdom to confess so much   100

66 come you] Q1; cam'st thou F   67 an it shall] Q1; so F   70 partition] Q1; perdition F   71 our own parts] Q1; my part F   71
like you now,] Q1; *not in* Q3   72 we] Q1; the Duke F   73–4 whelks . . . pimples] Q1; bubukles and whelkes, and knobs, and
flames a fire F   75 red . . . plue] Q1; plew . . . red F   75 God be praised] Q1; *not in* F   77 all] Q1; all such F   77 we here
give] Q1; here we give Q3; we give F   79 abused or upbraided] Q3 (abraided Q1); vpbraded or abused F   80 cruelty and
lenity] Q1; Leuitie and Crueltie F   80 gentlest . . . sooner] Q1; gentler . . . soonest F   81.1 *Enter*] Q1; *Enter the* Q3   83
we . . . we] Q1; I . . . I F   86 Go thee] Q1; Thus sayes my King: Say thou F   89 her folly] Q1; our folly Q2   89 her . . . her]
Q1; his . . . his F   89 rashness] Q1; weakenesse F   90–1 his army] Q1; the Muster of his Kingdome F   92 much from] Q1;
farre F   93 the . . . my] Q1; my . . . and F   94 We] Q1; I F   96 fair. Return] Q1; fairely. Turne F   98 well content] Q1;
willing F

Unto an enemy of craft and vantage,
My soldiers are with sickness much enfeebled,
My army lessened, and those few I have
Almost no better than so many French,
Who when they were in heart, I tell thee, herald,   105
I thought upon one pair of English legs
Did march three Frenchmen. Yet forgive me, God,
That I do brag thus. This your heir of France
Hath blown this vice in me. I must repent.
Go tell thy master here I am.   110
My ransom is this frail and worthless body,
My army but a weak and sickly guard.
Yet, God before, we will come on,
If France and such another neighbour stood in our way.
If we may pass, we will. If we be hindered,   115
We shall your tawny ground with your red blood discolour.
So, Montjoy, get you gone. There is for your pains.
The sum of all our answer is but this:
We would not seek a battle as we are,
Nor as we are, we say we will not shun it.   120

HERALD I shall deliver so. Thanks to your Majesty.

GLOUCESTER My Liege, I hope they will not come upon us now.

KING We are in God's hand, brother, not in theirs.
Tonight we will encamp beyond the bridge,
And on to morrow bid them march away.   125

                                                    [*Exeunt*]

[10] *Enter* BOURBON, CONSTABLE, ORLEANS, GEBON

CONSTABLE Tut, I have the best armour in the world.

ORLEANS You have an excellent armour, but let my horse have his due.

BOURBON Now you talk of a horse, I have a steed like the palfrey of the sun,
nothing but pure air and fire, and hath none of this dull element of earth
within him.   5

ORLEANS He is of the colour of the nutmeg.

BOURBON And of the heat a the ginger. Turn all the sands into eloquent
tongues, and my horse is argument for them all. I once writ a sonnet in the
praise of my horse, and began thus: 'Wonder of nature . . .'

102 soldiers] Q1; people F   103 army] Q1; numbers F   105 heart] Q1; health F   107 Frenchmen] F; Frenchmens Q1–
3   107 forgive me, God] Q1; God forgiue me Q3   108 heir] Q1; ayre F   109 this] Q1; that F   111 body] Q1; Trunke F   113
we] Q1; tell him we F   114 stood] Q1; Stand F   117 There is] Q1; there's Q3, F (There's)   117 pains] Q1; labour F   122
My Liege] Q1; *not in* F   122 now.] Q1; now? Q2   125 to morrow bid] Q1, F; tomorrow. Bid *Jackson*   **Scene 10**   0.1 GEBON]
Q1; *and Gebon* Q3   1 world.] Q1; World: would it were day. F   3 BOURBON] Q1; *Dolph.* F   7 a] Q1; of F   8 the] Q1; *not in*
Q2

CONSTABLE I have heard a sonnet begin so, in the praise of one's mistress.   10

BOURBON Why, then did they imitate that which I writ in praise of my horse, for my horse is my mistress.

CONSTABLE *Ma foy*, the other day, methought your mistress shook you shrewdly.

BOURBON Aye, bearing me. I tell thee, Lord Constable, my mistress wears her   15
own hair.

CONSTABLE I could make as good a boast of that if I had had a sow to my mistress.

BOURBON Tut, thou wilt make use of anything.

CONSTABLE Yet I do not use my horse for my mistress.   20

BOURBON Will it never be morning? I'll ride tomorrow a mile, and my way shall be paved with English faces.

CONSTABLE By my faith, so will not I, for fear I be outfaced of my way.

BOURBON Well, I'll go arm myself, hey!

                                                                   [*Exit*]

GEBON The Duke of Bourbon longs for morning.   25

ORLEANS Aye, he longs to eat the English.

CONSTABLE I think he'll eat all he kills.

ORLEANS Oh, peace. Ill will never said well.

CONSTABLE I'll cap that proverb with 'There is flattery in friendship'.

ORLEANS Oh sir, I can answer that, with 'Give the devil his due'.   30

CONSTABLE Have at the eye of that proverb with 'A jog of the devil'.

ORLEANS Well, the Duke of Bourbon is simply the most active gentleman of France.

CONSTABLE Doing his activity, and he'll still be doing.

ORLEANS He never did hurt as I heard of.   35

CONSTABLE No, I warrant you, nor never will.

ORLEANS I hold him to be exceeding valiant.

CONSTABLE I was told so by one that knows him better than you.

ORLEANS Who's that?

CONSTABLE Why, he told me so himself, and said he cared not who knew it.   40

ORLEANS Well, who will go with me to hazard for a hundred English prisoners?

CONSTABLE You must go to hazard yourself before you have them.

Enter a MESSENGER

MESSENGER My lords, the English lie within a hundred paces of your tent.

CONSTABLE Who hath measured the ground?   45

10 in the praise of] Q1; to F   11 writ] Q1; compos'd F   11 in praise . . . horse] Q1; to my Courser F   13–14 shook you shrewdly] Q1; shrewdly shooke your back F   15 her] Q1; his F   17 good] Q1; true F   21 morning] Q1; day F   21 ride] Q1; trot F   24 hey!] Q1; *not in* F   25 Duke of Bourbon] Q1; Dolphin F   26 Aye] Q1; *not in* F   28 Oh, peace] Q1; *not in* F   30 can answer] Q1; will take vp F   31 jog of] Q1; Pox of F   32 the Duke of Bourbon] Q1; He F   34 his] Q1; is F   35 hurt as] Q1; harme that F   37 hold] Q1; know F   38 so] Q1; that F   39 Who's that] Q1; What's hee F   40 Why] Q1; Marry F   41 go] Q1; first goe F   44 lords] Q1; Lord high Constable F

MESSENGER The Lord Grandpere.

CONSTABLE A valiant man, and an expert gentleman. Come, come, away! The
sun is high, and we wear out the day.

Exit omnes

[11] *Enter the* KING *disguised, to him* PISTOL

PISTOL *Qui va la?*

KING A friend.

PISTOL Discuss unto me, art thou gentleman? Or art thou common, base and
popular?

KING No sir, I am a gentleman of a company.   5

PISTOL Trails thou the puissant pike?

KING Even so, sir. What are you?

PISTOL As good a gentleman as the Emperor.

KING Oh, then thou art better than the King?

PISTOL The King's a bago, and a heart of gold, a lad of life, an imp of fame, of   10
parents good, of fist most valiant. I kiss his dirty shoe, and from my heart-
strings I love the lovely bully. What is thy name?

KING Harry le Roy.

PISTOL Le Roy, a Cornish man. Art thou of Cornish crew?

KING No sir, I am a Welshman.   15

PISTOL A Welshman. Knowst thou Llewellyn?

KING Aye sir, he is my kinsman.

PISTOL Art thou his friend?

KING Aye sir.

PISTOL *Figa* for thee then. My name is Pistol.   20

KING It sorts well with your fierceness.

PISTOL Pistol is my name.

Exit

Enter GOWER *and* LLEWELLYN

GOWER Captain Llewellyn!

LLEWELLYN In the name of Jesu, speak lower! It is the greatest folly in the
worell, when the ancient prerogatives of the wars be not kept. I warrant   25
you, if you look into the wars of the Romans you shall find no tittle-tattle
nor bibble-babble there, but you shall find the cares, and the fears, and the
ceremonies, to be otherwise.

GOWER Why, the enemy is loud. You heard him all night.

47 and an] Q2 (& an); a. an Q1; an Q3; most F   48 wear out] Q1; out-weare F   Scene 11   3 common, base] Q1; base,
common F   5 No sir] Q1; *not in* F   7 so, sir] Q1; so F   9 Oh,] Q1; *not in* F   10 bago] Q1; Bawcock F   10 a lad] F; *Pist.* A
lad Q1   12 my heart-strings] Q1; heartstring F   14 man] Q1; Name F   15 No sir] Q1; No F   16 A Welshman] Q1; *not in*
F   22 Pistol . . . name] Q1; *not in* F   24 Jesu] Q1, Q3; Ieshu Q2   24 lower] Q3; lewer Q1, Q2; fewer F   26 the Romans] Q1;
Pompey the Great F   27 fears] Q1; Formes F   29 heard] Q1; heare F

LLEWELLYN God's solud, if the enemy be an ass, and a fool, and a prating   30
    coxcomb, is it meet that we be also a fool, and a prating coxcomb, in your
    conscience now?
GOWER I'll speak lower.
LLEWELLYN I beseech you do, good Captain Gower.

                                                    Exit GOWER *and* LLEWELLYN

KING Though it appear a little out of fashion,   35
        Yet there's much care in this.

                            Enter three SOLDIERS

1 SOLDIER Is not that the morning yonder?
2 SOLDIER Aye, we see the beginning. God knows whether we shall see the end
    or no.
3 SOLDIER Well, I think the King could wish himself up to the neck in the   40
    middle of the Thames, and so I would he were, at all adventures, and I with
    him.
KING Now masters, good morrow, what cheer?
3 SOLDIER I'faith, small cheer some of us is like to have, ere this day end.
KING Why, fear nothing man, the King is frolic.   45
2 SOLDIER Aye, he may be, for he hath no such cause as we.
KING Nay, say not so, he is a man as we are. The violet smells to him as to us,
    therefore if he see reasons, he fears as we do.
2 SOLDIER But the King hath a heavy reckoning to make if his cause be not
    good, when all those souls whose bodies shall be slaughtered here shall join   50
    together at the latter day, and say 'I died at such a place', some swearing,
    some their wives rawly left, some leaving their children poor behind them.
    Now if his cause be bad, I think it will be a grievous matter to him.
KING Why, so you may say, if a man send his servant as factor into another
    country, and he by any means miscarry, you may say the business of the   55
    master was the author of his servant's misfortune. Or if a son be employed
    by his father, and he fall into any lewd action, you may say the father was
    the author of his son's damnation. But the master is not to answer for his
    servants, the father for his son, nor the King for his subjects. For they
    purpose not their deaths when they crave their services. Some there are   60
    that have the gift of premeditated murder on them, others the broken seal
    of forgery, in beguiling maidens. Now if these outstrip the law, yet they
    cannot escape God's punishment. War is God's beadle, war is God's
    vengeance. Every man's service is the King's, but every man's soul is
    his own. Therefore I would have every soldier examine himself, and wash   65

30 God's solud] Q1; *not in* F   36 this] Q1; this Welchman F   38–9 God knows . . . no] Q1; but I thinke wee shall neuer see the end of it F   44 day] Q1; day to an Q3   45 KING. . . . frolic] Q1; *not in* F   46 such] Q1; *not in* Q3   47 to] Q1; vnto Q3   50 souls . . . here] Q1; Legges, and Armes, and Heads, chopt off in a Battaile, F   52 rawly left] Q1; left poore behind F   52 left poor behind] Q1; rawly left F   60 deaths] Q1; death F   60 crave] Q1; purpose F; propose *Taylor*   61–2 seal of forgery] Q1; Seales of Periurie F   63 God's . . . God's] Q1; his . . . his F   64 man's] Q1; subject's F   64 service] Q1; Dutie F

every mote out of his conscience, that in so doing he may be the readier for
death; or not dying, why, the time was well spent wherein such preparation
was made.

3 SOLDIER I'faith, he says true: every man's fault on his own head. I would not
    have the King answer for me, yet I intend to fight lustily for him.   70

KING Well, I heard the King, he would not be ransomed.

2 SOLDIER Aye, he said so, to make us fight. But when our throats be cut he
    may be ransomed, and we never the wiser.

KING If I live to see that, I'll never trust his word again.

2 SOLDIER Mass, you'll pay him then! 'Tis a great displeasure that an elder gun   75
    can do against a cannon, or a subject against a monarch. You'll ne'er take
    his word again! You're an ass, go.

KING Your reproof is somewhat too bitter. Were it not at this time I could be
    angry.

2 SOLDIER Why let it be a quarrel if thou wilt.   80

KING How shall I know thee?

2 SOLDIER Here is my glove, which if ever I see in thy hat I'll challenge thee,
    and strike thee.

KING Here is likewise another of mine, and assure thee I'll wear it.

2 SOLDIER Thou dar'st as well be hanged.   85

3 SOLDIER Be friends, you fools. We have French quarrels enough in hand; we
    have no need of English broils.

KING 'Tis no treason to cut French crowns, for tomorrow the King himself will
    be a clipper.

                                Exit the SOLDIERS

    O God of battles, steel my soldiers' hearts!   90
    Take from them now the sense of reckoning,
    That the opposéd multitudes which stand before them
    May not appal their courage. Oh, not today,
    Not today, O God, think on the fault
    My father made in compassing the crown.   95
    I Richard's body have interréd new,
    And on it have bestowed more contrite tears
    Than from it issued forcéd drops of blood.
    A hundred men have I in yearly pay,
    Which every day their withered hands hold up   100
    To heaven to pardon blood.

66 mote] Q1 (moath); Moth F   71 king, he would] Q1; king wold Q3   72 be] Q1; are F   74 that] Q1; it F   74 again] Q1; after
F   75 Mass] Q1; *not in* F   77 you're an ass, go] Q2 (you are an asse goe); your a nasse goe Q1; you are a nasse, goe Q3; *not
in* F   78 somewhat too bitter] Q1; something too round F   80 thou wilt] Q1; you liue F   82 Here is] Q1; here's Q3   84 and
assure] Q1; and ile assure Q2   86 enough] F (enow); anow Q1   86–7 in hand . . . broils] Q1; if you could tell how to reckon
F   88 for] Q1; and F   89.1 *Exit the* SOLDIERS Q1; *at line* 87 F   89.2 *Enter the King, Gloster, Epingam, and Attendants.* Q1;
Enter to the King Q3; *not in* F   92 That] Q1; of F; ere *Moore Smith*; if *Stevens*; or *Wilson*   94 O God] Q1; O Lord F   94 think
on] Q1; thinke not vpon F   97 have] F; hath Q1   99 have I] Q1; I haue F   100 which every] Q1; Who twice a F   101 To]
Q1; Toward F

And I have built two chantries. More will I do,
Though all that I can do is all too little.

Enter GLOSTER

GLOSTER My Lord!
KING My brother Gloster's voice.   105
GLOSTER My Lord, the army stays upon your presence.
KING Stay, Gloster, stay, and I will go with thee.
        The day, my friends, and all things stay for me.

                                                              [*Exeunt*]

[12] *Enter* CLARENCE, GLOSTER, EXETER, *and* SALISBURY [*and* WARWICK]

WARWICK My lords, the French are very strong.
EXETER There is five to one, and yet they all are fresh.
WARWICK Of fighting men they have full forty thousand.
SALISBURY The odds is all too great. Farewell, kind lords.
        Brave Clarence, and my Lord of Gloster,   5
        My Lord of Warwick, and to all farewell.
CLARENCE Farewell, kind Lord. Fight valiantly today.
        And yet in truth I do thee wrong,
        For thou art made on the true sparks of honour.

Enter KING

WARWICK Oh, would we had but ten thousand men   10
        Now at this instant that doth not work in England!
KING Who's that that wishes so? My cousin Warwick?
        God's will, I would not lose the honour
        One man would share from me,
        Not for my kingdom.   15
        No, faith, my cousin, wish not one man more.
        Rather proclaim it presently through our camp
        That he that hath no stomach to this feast
        Let him depart; his passport shall be drawn,
        And crowns for convoy put into his purse.   20
        We would not die in that man's company
        That fears his fellowship to die with us.
        This day is called the day of Crispin.

102 chantries] F; chanceries Q1; Chanceries Q2, Q3   103 all too little] Q1; nothing worth F   108 stay] F; stayes Q1–
3   **Scene 12**   1 WARWICK ... strong] Q1; *not in* F   2 There is] Q1; There's Q3   3 forty] Q1; threescore F   7 kind Lord]
Q1; kind lords Q3; good *Salisbury* F   9 made on ... honour] Q1; fram'd of the firme truth of valour F   10 ten thousand]
Q1; one ten thousand of those F   12 Who's that] Q1; What's he F   12 Warwick] Q1; *Westmerland* F   14 One man] Q1; As
one man more me thinkes F   15 Not ... kingdom] Q1; For the best hope I haue F   17 presently] Q1; (*Westmerland*) F   17
our camp] Q1; my hoast F   18 feast] Q1; fight F   19 drawn] Q1; made F   23 day] Q1; Feast F   23 Crispin] Q1; Crispian F

He that outlives this day and sees old age
Shall stand a-tiptoe when this day is named,   25
And rouse him at the name of Crispin.
He that outlives this day, and comes safe home,
Shall yearly on the vigil feast his friends,
And say, 'Tomorrow is Saint Crispin's Day!'
Then shall we in their flowing bowls   30
Be newly remembered. Harry the King,
Bedford and Exeter, Clarence and Gloster,
Warwick and York,
Familiar in their mouths as household words.
This story shall the good man tell his son,   35
And from this day unto the general doom
But we in it shall be rememberéd.
We few, we happy few, we bond of brothers –
For he today that sheds his blood by mine
Shall be my brother – be he ne'er so base   40
This day shall gentle his condition.
Then shall he strip his sleeves and show his scars,
And say, 'These wounds I had on Crispin's Day'.
And gentlemen in England now abed
Shall think themselves accurst,   45
And hold their manhood cheap,
While any speak that fought with us
Upon Saint Crispin's Day.

GLOSTER My gracious lord, the French is in the field.
KING Why, all things are ready if our minds be so.   50
WARWICK Perish the man whose mind is backward now!
KING Thou dost not wish more help from England, cousin?
WARWICK God's will, my Liege, would you and I alone,
      Without more help, might fight this battle out.
KING Why, well said. That doth please me better   55
      Than to wish me one. You know your charge.
      God be with you all.

Enter the HERALD *from the French*

HERALD Once more I come to know of thee, King Henry,
      What thou wilt give for ransom?

24 sees . . . age] Q1; comes safe home F   26 Crispin] Q1; Crispian F   27 outlives] Q1; shall see F   27 comes . . . home]
Q1; liue old age F   28 friends] Q1; neighbours F   29 Crispin's Day] Q1; Crispian F   32 Clarence and Gloster] Q1; *Warwick*
and Talbot F   33 Warwick and York] Q1; *Salisbury and Gloucester* F   34 their mouths] Q1; his mouth F   35 tell] Q1;
teach F   36 general doom] Q1; ending of the World F   38 bond] Q1; band F   39 by mine] Q1; with me F   40 base] Q1; vile
F   43 And . . . Day'] Q1; *not in* F   45–7 accurst . . . While] Q1; accurst, / they were not there, when Q3   46 manhood]
Q1; Manhoods F   49 GLOSTER] Q1; *Sal.* F   50 Why,] Q1; *not in* F   54 battle out] Q1; Royall battaile F   55 *Kin.*] Q2, F;
not in Q1, Q3   55 well . . . better] Q1; now thou hast vnwisht fiue thousand men: / Which likes me better F   56 me] Q1;
vs F   56 charge] Q1; places F   58 Henry] Q1; *Harry* F   59 What . . . ransom] Q1; If for thy Ransome thou wilt now
compound F

KING Who hath sent thee now?   60
HERALD The Constable of France.
KING I prithee bear my former answer back.
    Bid them achieve me, and then sell my bones.
    Good God, why should they mock good fellows thus?
    The man that once did sell the lion's skin   65
    While the beast lived was killed with hunting him.
    A many of our bodies shall no doubt
    Find graves within your realm of France.
    Though buried in your dunghills we shall be famed,
    For there the sun shall greet them   70
    And draw up their honours reeking up to heaven,
    Leaving their earthly parts to choke your clime,
    The smell whereof shall breed a plague in France.
    Mark then abundant valour in our English,
    That being dead, like to the bullet's crazing   75
    Breaks forth into a second course of mischief,
    Killing in relapse of mortality.
    Let me speak proudly:
    There's not a piece of feather in our camp,
    Good argument, I hope, we shall not fly;   80
    And time hath worn us into slovenry,
    But by the Mass our hearts are in the trim,
    And my poor soldiers tell me yet ere night
    They'll be in fresher robes, or they will pluck
    The gay new clothes o'er your French soldiers' ears, 85
    And turn them out of service. If they do this,
    As if it please God they shall,
    Then shall our ransom soon be levied.
    Save thou thy labour, herald.
    Come thou no more for ransom, gentle herald.   90
    They shall have nought, I swear, but these my bones,
    Which if they have, as I will leave 'em them,
    Will yield them little. Tell the Constable.
HERALD I shall deliver so.
                              Exit HERALD
YORK My gracious lord, upon my knee I crave   95
    The leading of the vaward.
KING Take it, brave York. Come, soldiers, let's away,
    And as thou pleasest, God, dispose the day.
                                  Exit

64 good] Q1; poore F   67 A many] Q1, F; And many Q3   68 graves] Q1; Natiue Graues F   69 we] Q1; They F   71 draw up] Q1; draw F   74 abundant] Q1; abounding F   76 Breaks forth] Q1; Breake out F   79 camp] Q1; Hoast F   80 shall] Q1; will F   82 are in the trim] Q1; within are trim Q2   85 clothes] Q1; Coats F   85 your] Q1; the F   85 ears] Q1; heads F   88 Then . . . ransom] Q1; my Ransome then / Will F   88 soon be] Q1; be Q2   91 nought] Q1; none F   91 bones] Q1; ioynts F   95 gracious lord] Q1; Lord F   97 Come] Q1; Now F   92 as] Q1; how F

[13] *Enter the four French lords* [GEBON, CONSTABLE, ORLEANS, BOURBON]

GEBON Oh, *diabolo*!
CONSTABLE *Mort de ma vie*!
ORLEANS Oh, what a day is this!
BOURBON *O jour des heures*! All is gone, all is lost!
CONSTABLE We are enough yet living in the field   5
        To smother up the English,
        If any order might be thought upon.
BOURBON A plague of order! Once more to the field,
        And he that will not follow Bourbon now,
        Let him go home, and with his cap in hand,   10
        Like a base leno hold the chamber door,
        Why, lest by a slave no gentler than my dog
        His fairest daughter is contaminate.
CONSTABLE Disorder, that hath spoiled us, right us now!
        Come we in heaps, we'll offer up our lives   15
        Unto these English, or else die with fame.
        Come, come along,
        Let's die with honour, our shame doth last too long!

                                  Exit omnes

[14] *Enter* PISTOL, *the* FRENCH *man, and the* BOY

PISTOL Yield cur, yield cur!
FRENCH *O Monsieur, je vous en prie, avez pitié de moi*!
PISTOL 'Moy' shall not serve, I will have forty moys. Boy, ask him his
        name.
BOY *Comment êtes-vous appelé*?   5
FRENCH *Monsieur Fer*.
BOY He says his name is Master Fer.
PISTOL I'll Fer him, and ferret him, and firk him! Boy, discuss the same in
        French.
BOY Sir, I do not know what's French for fer, ferret and firk't.   10
PISTOL Bid him prepare, for I will cut his throat.
BOY *Faites-vous prier: il voulais coupler votre gorge*.
PISTOL *Ah, oui! Ma foi! Couplez la gorge!* Unless thou give to me egregious
        ransom, die, on point of a fox!

Scene 13   2 *Mort de*] Q1 (Mor du); *Mor Dieu* F   6 English] Q1; English in our throngs F   8 the] Q1; *not in* Q2   10 home]
Q1; hence F   11 leno] Q1; Pander F   12 lest . . . slave] Q1; Whilst a base slaue F; Whilst by a slave *Pope*   13 contaminate]
F (contaminated); contamuracke Q1   14 right] Q1; friend F   18 Let's . . . long] Q1; Let life be short, else shame will be too
long F   **Scene 14**   1 Yield . . . cur!] Q1 (Eyld cur, eyld cur.); Yeeld Curre. F   3 him] Q1; *not in* Q3   10 firk't] Q1 (fearkt);
ferke Q2; fearke Q3; firke F   14 die, on point of a fox!] Q1 (dye. / One poynt of a foxe.); dye. / *One point of a Foxe*. Q2; dye.
/ One poynt of a foxe. Q3; on point of Fox F

FRENCH *Que dit-il, monsieur?*   15
BOY *Il dite, si vous ne voulez pas donner lui la grande ransome: il vous tuerez.*
FRENCH *Oh! Je vous en prie, petit gentilhomme, parlez a ce grand captaine pour*
    avez merci a moi, et je donnerai pour mon ransome cinquante écus. Je suis un
    gentilhomme de France.   20
PISTOL What says he, boy?
BOY Marry, sir, he says he is a gentleman of a great house of France, and for his
    ransom he will give you five hundred crowns.
PISTOL My fury shall abate, and I the crowns will take, and as I suck blood,
    I will some mercy show. Follow me, cur.   25

                                                                    Exit omnes

[15] *Enter the* KING, *and his nobles* [EXETER, WARWICK, GLOSTER], PISTOL

KING What, the French retire?
        Yet all is not done, yet keep the French the field.
EXETER The Duke of York commends him to your Grace.
KING Lives he, good uncle? Twice I saw him down,
        Twice up again,   5
        From helmet to the spur, all bleeding o'er.
EXETER In which array, brave soldier, doth he lie,
        Larding the plains, and by his bloody side,
        Yoke-fellow to his honour-dying wounds,
        The noble Earl of Suffolk also lies.   10
        Suffolk first died, and York, all hasted o'er,
        Comes to him where in blood he lay steeped,
        And takes him by the beard, kisses the gashes
        That bloodily did yawn upon his face,
        And cried aloud, 'Tarry, dear cousin Suffolk!   15
        My soul shall thine keep company in heaven.
        Tarry dear soul awhile, then fly to rest.
        And in this glorious and well-foughten field
        We kept together in our chivalry'.
        Upon these words I came and cheered them up.   20
        He took me by the hand, said 'Dear my lord,
        Commend my service to my sovereign'.
        So did he turn, and over Suffolk's neck

16 Boy *Il dite . . . la*] This edn; Ill dityе . . . *Boy. La* Q1   16 *donner*] This edn; domy Q1   19 *cinquante écus*] Q1; *deux cents escus* F   23 five hundred] Q1 (500); two hundred F   Scene 15   1 What . . . retire?] Q1; Well haue we done, thrice-valiant Countrimen, F   2 Yet all] Q1; But all F   2 all is] Q1; als Q3; all's F   2 yet keep . . . the] Q1; the French keepes still the Q3   3 Grace] Q1; Maiesty F   6 bleeding o'er] Q1; blood he was F   9 honour-dying] Q1; honour-owing F   10 also] Q1; *not in* Q2   11 hasted] Q1; wounded Q3; hagled ouer F   12 blood] Q1; gore F   12 lay] Q1; lay all Q3   12 steeped] Q1; insteeped F   14 yawn] F; yane Q1   15 And cried] Q1; He cryes F   17 dear] Q1; sweet F   17 awhile] Q1; for mine F   17 to rest] Q1; a-brest F   18 And] Q1; As F   20 them] Q1; him F

He threw his wounded arm, and, so espoused to death,
With blood he sealed an argument   25
Of never-ending love. The pretty and sweet manner of it
Forced those waters from me which I would have stopped,
But I had not so much of man in me
But all my mother came into my eyes,
And gave me up to tears.

KING   I blame you not,   30
For hearing you, I must convert to tears.

Alarum sounds

What new alarum is this? Bid every soldier kill his prisoner.
PISTOL *Couple gorge!*

Exit omnes

[16] *Enter* LLEWELLYN *and Captain* GOWER

LLEWELLYN God's plood! Kill the boys and the luggage! 'Tis the arrantest
piece of knavery as can be desired, in the worell now, in your conscience
now!

GOWER 'Tis certain, there is not a boy left alive, and the cowardly rascals that
ran from the battle, themselves have done this slaughter. Beside, they have   5
carried away and burned all that was in the King's tent, whereupon the
King caused every prisoner's throat to be cut. Oh, he is a worthy king!

LLEWELLYN Aye, he was born at Monmouth. Captain Gower, what call you
the place where Alexander the big was born?

GOWER Alexander the Great.   10

LLEWELLYN Why, I pray, is nat big great? As if I say, big or great, or magnanimous, I hope it is all one reckoning, save the phrase is a little variation.

GOWER I think Alexander the Great was born at Macedon. His father was
called Philip of Macedon, as I take it.

LLEWELLYN I think it was Macedon indeed where Alexander was born. Look   15
you, Captain Gower, an if you look into the maps of the worell well you
shall find little difference between Macedon and Monmouth. Look you,
there is a river in Macedon, and there is also a river in Monmouth. The
river's name at Monmouth is called Wye, but 'tis out of my brain what is
the name of the other. But 'tis all one, 'tis so like as my fingers is to my   20

25 argument] Q1; Testament F   26 never-ending] Q1; Noble-ending F   28 I had not] Q3, F; I not Q1, Q2   29 But] Q1; And
F   31 you] Q1; this F   31 convert to tears] Q1; perforce compound / With mixtfull eyes F   32 Bid] Q1; Then F   32
prisoner] Q1; prisoners F   33 PISTOL.. *Couple gorge*] Q1; *not in* F   **Scene 16**   1 arrantest] This edn; atrants Q1; arrants Q3;
as arrant a F   8 Monmouth] Q3, F; *Monmorth* Q1, Q2   10 Great.] F; great. Q1; great? Q2; great. Q3   12 it is] Q1; tis Q3   12
variation] Q1; variations F   15 was . . . indeed] Q1; is in *Macedon* F; is e'en Macedon *Oxford*   19 brain] Q1; praines F   20
other] Q1; other Riuer F   20 to my] Q1; to Q3

fingers, and there is salmons in both. Look you, Captain Gower, an you
mark it, you shall find our King is come after Alexander. God knows, and
you know, that Alexander, in his bowls, and his ales, and his wrath, and his
displeasures and indignations, was kill his friend Clitus.

GOWER Aye, but our King is not like him in that, for he never killed any of his   25
friends.

LLEWELLYN Look you, 'tis not well done to take the tale out of a man's mouth
e'er it is made an end and finished. I speak in the comparisons: as Alexander is kill his friend Clitus, so our King, being in his ripe wits and judgements, is turn away the fat knight with the great belly doublet. I am forget   30
his name.

GOWER Sir John Falstaff.

LLEWELLYN Aye, I think it is Sir John Falstaff indeed. I can tell you, there's
good men born at Monmouth.

Enter KING *and the Lords* [*and* 2 SOLDIER]

KING I was not angry since I came into France   35
　　　Until this hour. Take a trumpet, herald,
　　　And ride unto the horsemen on yon hill.
　　　If they will fight with us bid them come down,
　　　Or leave the field; they do offend our sight.
　　　Will they do neither, we will come to them,   40
　　　And make them skir away as fast
　　　As stones enforced from the old Assyrian slings.
　　　Besides, we'll cut the throats of those we have,
　　　And not one alive shall taste our mercy.

Enter the HERALD

　　　God's will, what means this? Knowst thou not   45
　　　That we have fined these bones of ours for ransom?

HERALD I come, great King, for charitable favour,
　　　To sort our nobles from our common men.
　　　We may have leave to bury all our dead,
　　　Which in the field lie spoiled and trodden on.   50

KING I tell thee truly, herald, I do not know whether
　　　The day be ours or no,
　　　For yet a many of your French do keep the field.

---

22 come . . . Alexander] Q1; come after it indifferent well F   23 bowls . . . ales] Q1 (alles); rages, and his furies F   25 for he]
Q1; he F   27 Look you] Q1; *not in* F   28 made . . . finished] Q1; made and finished F   29 is kill] Q1; kild F   30 is turn] Q1;
turn'd F   30 am forget] Q1; haue forgot F   34.1 *the Lords*] Q1; *his Lords* Q3; *Alarum. Enter King Harry and Burbon with
prisoners. Flourish* F   35 into] Q1; in Q3; to F   36 hour] Q1; instant F   37 And ride] Q1; Ride thou F   39 leave] Q1; voyde
F   41 fast] Q1; swift F   44 one alive] Q1; a man of them that we shall take F   45 God's will] Q1; How now F   46
we . . . ours] Q1; I . . . mine F   47 favour] Q1; License F   49 We . . . dead] Q1; That we may wander ore this bloody field,
/ To booke our dead, and then to bury them F   50 Which . . . on] Q1; *not in* F   51 do not know] Q1; know not F   53 yet
a many] Q1; yet many Q2   53 French . . . the] Q1; horsemen peere, / And gallop ore the F

HERALD The day is yours.

KING Praised be God therefore.   55
       What castle call you that?

HERALD We call it Agincourt.

KING Then call we this the field of Agincourt,
       Fought on the day of Crispin, Crispin.

LLEWELLYN Your grandfather of famous memory, if your grace be remem-   60
      bered, is do good service in France.

KING 'Tis true, Llewellyn.

LLEWELLYN Your Majesty says very true. An it please your Majesty, the
      Welshmen there was do good service, in a garden where leeks did grow.
      And I think your Majesty will take no scorn to wear a leek in your cap upon   65
      Saint Davy's Day.

KING No, Llewellyn, for I am Welsh as well as you.

LLEWELLYN All the water in Wye will not wash your Welsh blood out of you,
      God keep it and preserve it, to his Grace's will and pleasure.

KING Thanks, good countryman.   70

LLEWELLYN By Jesus, I am your Majesty's countryman. I care not who know
      it, so long as your Majesty is an honest man.

KING God keep me so. Our herald go with him,
      And bring us the number of the scattered French.

                                    Exit Heralds

      Call yonder soldier hither.   75

LLEWELLYN You fellow, come to the King.

KING Fellow, why dost thou wear that glove in thy hat?

2 SOLDIER An't please your Majesty, 'tis a rascal's that swaggered with me the
      other day; and he hath one of mine, which if ever I see, I have sworn to
      strike him. So hath he sworn the like to me.   80

KING How think you, Llewellyn, is it lawful he keep his oath?

LLEWELLYN An it please your majesty, 'tis lawful he keep his vow. If he be
      perjured once, he is as arrant a beggarly knave as treads upon two black
      shoes.

KING His enemy may be a gentleman of worth.   85

LLEWELLYN An if he be as good a gentleman as Lucifer and Beelzebub, and
      the devil himself, 'tis meet he keep his vow.

KING Well, sirrah, keep your word.
      Under what captain servest thou?

57 We] Q1; They F   59 Crispin, Crispin] Q1; Crispin, Crispianus Q3; Crispin Crispianus F   62 'Tis true] Q1; They did
F   65 will take no scorn] Q1; wil not scorne Q2; takes no scorne F   68 you] Q1; your pody F   70 good countryman] Q1; good
my countrymen F   71 Jesus] Q1; Iesu Q3; Ieshu F   73 God] Q1; Good F   73 herald] Q1; Heralds F   74 us ... French] Q1;
me iust notice of the numbers dead/ On both our parts F   75 soldier] Q1; fellow F   76 fellow] Q1; Souldier F   77 Fellow]
Q1; Souldier F   77 hat] Q1; Cappe F   80 he sworn] Q1; he Q3   82 lawful he] Q1; fit this souldier F   85 worth] Q1; great
sort F

2 SOLDIER Under Captain Gower.   90

LLEWELLYN Captain Gower is a good captain, and hath good literature in the
wars.

KING Go call him hither.

2 SOLDIER I will, my lord.

Exit 2 SOLDIER

KING Captain Llewellyn, when Alençon and I was down together, I took this   95
glove off from his helmet. Here, Llewellyn, wear it. If any do challenge it,
he is a friend of Alençon's, and an enemy to me.

LLEWELLYN Your Majesty doth me as great a favour as can be desired in the
hearts of his subjects. I would see that man now that should challenge this
glove. An it please God of His grace, I would but see him, that is all.   100

KING Llewellyn, knowest thou Captain Gower?

LLEWELLYN Captain Gower is my friend. An if it like your Majesty, I know
him very well.

KING Go call him hither.

LLEWELLYN I will, an it shall please your Majesty.   105

[*Exit*]

KING [*To* WARWICK] Follow Llewellyn closely at the heels.
The glove he wears, it was the soldier's.
It may be there will be harm between them,
For I do know Llewellyn valiant,
And being touched, as hot as gunpowder,   110
And quickly will return an injury.
Go see there be no harm between them.

[*Exeunt*]

[**17**] *Enter* GOWER, LLEWELLYN, *and the* 2 SOLDIER

LLEWELLYN Captain Gower, in the name of Jesu, come to his Majesty. There
is more good toward you than you can dream of.

2 SOLDIER Do you hear, you sir? Do you know this glove?

LLEWELLYN I know the glove is a glove.

2 SOLDIER Sir, I know this, and thus I challenge it.   5

He strikes him

LLEWELLYN God plut, and his. Captain Gower, stand away! I'll give treason
his due presently.

Enter the KING, WARWICK, CLARENCE, *and* EXETER

91–2 hath . . . literature] Q1; is good knowledge and literatured F   96 was] Q1–2; were Q3, F   96 from his] Q1; from's
Q3   96 helmet] Q1; helme F   96 any do] Q1; any Q3   99 that should] Q1; that wold Q3   107 was] Q1; is F   **Scene 17**   2
toward] Q1; towards Q3   3 2 SOLDIER] Q1 (*Soul.*); *Flew.* Q2   3 Do . . . sir?] Q1; *not in* F   4 the] Q2; the the Q1   6 God plut,
and his] Q1 (Gode); 'Sblud F

KING How now, what is the matter?

LLEWELLYN An it shall please your Majesty, here is the notablest piece of
treason come to light as you shall desire to see in a summer's day. Here is   10
a rascal, beggarly rascal is strike the glove which your Majesty took out of
the helmet of Alençon, and your Majesty will bear me witness, and testi-
mony, and avouchments, that this is the glove.

2 SOLDIER An it please your Majesty, that was my glove. He that I gave it to in
the night promised me to wear it in his hat. I promised to strike him if he   15
did. I met that gentleman, with my glove in his hat, and I think I have been
as good as my word.

LLEWELLYN Your Majesty hears, under your Majesty's manhood, what a
beggarly lousy knave it is.

KING Let me see thy glove. Look you,   20
    This is the fellow of it.
    It was I indeed you promised to strike.
    And thou hast given me most bitter words.
    How canst thou make us amends?

LLEWELLYN Let his neck answer it, if there be any marshal's law in the worell!   25

2 SOLDIER My Liege, all offences come from the heart. Never came any from
mine to offend your Majesty. You appeared to me as a common man:
witness the night, your garments, your lowliness; and whatsoever you
received under that habit, I beseech your Majesty impute it to your own
fault, and not mine. For your self came not like yourself. Had you been as   30
you seemed, I had made no offence. Therefore I beseech your Grace to
pardon me.

KING Uncle, fill the glove with crowns,
    And give it to the soldier. Wear it, fellow,
    As an honour in thy cap, till I do challenge it.   35
    Give him the crowns. Come, Captain Llewellyn,
    I must needs have you friends.

LLEWELLYN By Jesus, the fellow hath mettle enough in his belly. Hark you,
soldier, there is a shilling for you, and keep yourself out of brawls and
brabbles, and dissentions, and, look you, it shall be the better for you.   40

2 SOLDIER I'll none of your money, sir, not I.

LLEWELLYN Why, 'tis a good shilling, man. Why should you be squeamish?
    Your shoes are not so good, it will serve you to mend your shoes.

8 what is] Q1; Whats Q3   9 An it . . . Majesty] Q1; My Liege F   11 took] Q1; in person tooke Q3   12 testimony] Q1;
testimonies Q3   14 An . . . Majesty] Q1; My Liege F   16 that gentleman] Q1; this man F   16 in his] Q1; in's Q3   16 hat]
Q1; Cappe F   16 I think I] Q1; I F   20 Let . . . glove] Q1; Giue me thy Gloue Souldier F   20–1 Look you, This] Q1; Looke,
heere F   22 you] Q1; thou F   23 thou] Q2; thou thou Q1   24 us] Q1; me F   25 be any marshal's] Q1; is any Marshall F   27
as] Q1; but as Q3   28–9 whatsoever . . . received] Q1; what your Highnesse suffer'd F   29 your . . . impute] Q1; you take
F   30 not] Q1; not to Q3   31 seemed,] Q1; seemed then to me, Q3   31 Grace to] Q1; Highnesse F   34 the soldier] Q1; this
fellow F   34–5 Wear . . . As] Q1; Keepe . . . And weare it for F   38 By Jesus] Q1; By this Day and this Light F   38 Hark
you] Q1; Hold F   39 shilling] Q1; silling Q3; twelue pence F   40 look you] Q1; I warrant you F   41 sir, not I] Q1; *not in*
F   42 shilling] Q1; silling Q3   42 squeamish] Q1; so pashfull F   43 it . . . shoes] Q1; 'tis a good silling I warrant you, or I
will change it F

KING What men of sort are taken, uncle?

EXETER Charles, Duke of Orleans, nephew to the King.   45
      John, Duke of Bourbon, and Lord Bouchequal.
      Of other lords and barons, knights and squires,
      Full fifteen hundred, besides common men.

KING This note doth tell me of ten thousand
      French, that in the field lies slain.   50
      Of nobles bearing banners in the field,
      Charles de la Brute, High Constable of France,
      Jaques of Chattilion, Admiral of France,
      The Master of the Crossbows, John, Duke Alençon,
      Lord Rambures, High Master of France,   55
      The brave Sir Guiscard Dauphin, of Nobelle Charillas,
      Granpré, and Rossy, Faulconbridge and Foi,
      Gerard and Verton, Vandemont and Lestra.
      Here was a royal fellowship of death.
      Where is the number of our English dead?   60
      Edward, the Duke of York, the Earl of Suffolk,
      Sir Richard Ketly, Davy Gam esquire,
      And of all other, but five and twenty.
      Oh God, Thy arm was here,
      And unto Thee alone ascribe we praise.   65
      When without strategem,
      And in even shock of battle, was ever heard
      So great and little loss, on one part and another.
      Take it, God, for it is only Thine.

EXETER 'Tis wonderful.   70

KING Come, let us go on procession through the camp.
      Let it be death proclaimed to any man
      To boast hereof, or take the praise from God,
      Which is His due.

LLEWELLYN Is it lawful, an it please your Majesty, to tell how many is killed?   75

KING Yes, Llewellyn, but with this acknowledgement,
      That God fought for us.

LLEWELLYN Yes, in my conscience, He did us great good.

KING Let there be sung *Non Nobis* and *Te Deum*.
      The dead with charity interred in clay.   80

---

44 men of] Q1; Prisoners of good F   49 KING] F; *not in* Q1–3   51 nobles . . . field] Q1; Princes in this number, / And Nobles bearing Banners F   52 de la Brute] Q1; *Delabreth* F   52 Constable] Q1; Constanble Q3   55 High] Q1; Great F   56 Sir Guiscard . . . Charillas] sir *Gwigzard, Dolphin.*Of *Nobelle Charillas*, Q1–3; Sir *Guichard Dolphin* F   59 Here was] Q1; *King.* Here was Q2; *King.* Heeres Q3   62] Q1; *not in* Q2   65 unto Thee alone] Q1; not to vs, but to thy Arme alone F   65 praise] Q1; all F   67 And in] Q1; But in plain shock, and F   67 in even] Q1; euen in Q3   67 heard] Q1; knowne F   68 another] Q1; on th'other F   69 it God] Q1; it O God Q3   69 only] Q1; none but F   71 let . . . on] Q1; goe me in F   72 Let it be] Q1; And be it F   72 to any man] Q1; through our Hoast F   73 hereof] Q1; of this F   74 due] Q1; onely F   75 lawful] Q1; not lawfull F   76 Llewellyn] Q1 (*Flewellen*); Captaine F   80 interred] Q1 (enterred); enter'd Q3; enclos'd F

We'll then to Calais, and to England then,
Where ne'er from France arrived more happier men.

                                                                      Exit omnes

[18]   *Enter* GOWER *and* LLEWELLYN

GOWER   But why do you wear your leek today? Saint Davy's Day is past.
LLEWELLYN   There is occasion, Captain Gower. Look you why, and where-
    fore. The other day, look you, Pistol, which you know is a man of no merits
    in the worell, is come where I was the other day, and brings bread and salt,
    and bids me eat my leek. 'Twas in a place, look you, where I could move no   5
    dissentions, but if I can see him, I shall tell him a little of my desires.
GOWER   Here a comes, swelling like a turkey-cock.

                              Enter PISTOL

LLEWELLYN   'Tis no matter for his swelling, and his turkey-cocks. God pless
    you, Ancient Pistol, you scald, beggarly, lousy knave, God pless you.
PISTOL   Ha, art thou bedlam? Dost thou thirst, base Trojan, to have me fold up   10
    Parca's fatal web? Hence, I am qualmish at the smell of leek.
LLEWELLYN   Ancient Pistol, I would desire you, because it doth not agree with
    your stomach, and your appetite, and your digestions, to eat this leek.
PISTOL   Not for Cadwallader and all his goats!
LLEWELLYN   There is one goat for you, Ancient Pistol.   15

                          He strikes him

PISTOL   Base Trojan, thou shall die!
LLEWELLYN   Aye, I know I shall die. Meantime, I would desire you to live and
    eat this leek.
GOWER   Enough, Captain, you have astonished him.
LLEWELLYN   Astonished him! By Jesu, I'll beat his head four days and four   20
    nights but I'll make him eat some part of my leek.
PISTOL   Well, must I bite?
LLEWELLYN   Aye, out of question, or doubt, or ambiguities, you must bite.

                  He makes Ancient Pistol bite of the leek

PISTOL   Good, good.
LLEWELLYN   Aye, leeks are good, Ancient Pistol. There is a shilling for you to   25
    heal your bloody coxcomb.

81 We'll] Q1; And F   82 happier] Q1; happy F   **Scene 18**   1 But] Q1; Nay, that's right: but F   5–6 move . . . dissentions]
Q1; breed no contention F   7 a comes] Q1; he comes Q3, F   13 stomach] Q1; stomackes Q3   13 appetite] Q1; appetites
Q3   17 Aye . . . die] Q1; You say very true, scauld knaue, when Gods will is F   17 Meantime,] Q1; but in the meane time
Q3   19 astonished him] Q1; astonished him, it is enough Q3   20 Astonished . . . Jesu] Q1; I say, F   21 nights] Q1; nights
too, Q3   23 Aye] Q1; Yes certainly F   23 you . . . bite] Q1; *not in* F   23.1 *He . . . leek*] Q3; not in Q1–2, F   24 Good, good]
Q1; Good F   25 Ancient Pistol] Q1; hold you F   25 There] Q1; Looke you now, there Q3   25 shilling] Q1; groat F

PISTOL Me a shilling!

LLEWELLYN If you will not take it, I have another leek for you.

PISTOL I take thy shilling in earnest of reckoning.

LLEWELLYN If I owe you anything, I'll pay you in cudgels. You shall be a   30
   woodmonger, and buy cudgels. God be wi' you, Ancient Pistol, God bless
   you, and heal your broken pate. Ancient Pistol, if you see leeks another
   time, mock at them, that is all. God be wi' you.

                                                 Exit LLEWELLYN [*and* GOWER]

PISTOL All hell shall stir for this!
         Doth Fortune play the hussy with me now?   35
         Is honour cudgelled from my warlike lines?
         Well, France farewell. News have I certainly
         That Doll is sick. One malady of France.
         The wars affordeth nought, home will I trudge.
         Bawd will I turn, and use the sleight of hand.   40
         To England will I steal, and there I'll steal,
         And patches will I get unto these scars,
         And swear I got them in the Gallia wars.

                                                                   Exit PISTOL

[19] *Enter at one door the* KING *of England and his Lords* [EXETER]. *And at the*
other door, the FRENCH KING, *Queen* [*Princess*] KATHERINE, [ALICE], *the Duke of*
BURGUNDY [BOURBON], *and others*

KING Peace to this meeting, wherefore we are met.
         And to our brother France, fair time of day.
         Fair health unto our lovely cousin Katherine.
         And, as a branch and member of this stock,
         We do salute you, Duke of Burgundy.   5

FRENCH KING Brother of England, right joyous are we to behold
         Your face; so are we princes English every one.

BURGUNDY With pardon unto both your mightiness,
         Let it not displease you if I demand
         What rub or bar hath thus far hindered you,   10
         To keep you from the gentle speech of peace?

KING If, Duke of Burgundy, you would have peace,
         You must buy that peace,
         According as we have drawn our Articles.

27 shilling] Q1; groat F   29 shilling] Q1; groat F   29 reckoning] Q1; reuenge F   30 I'll] Q1 (ile); I will Q3   31 buy] Q3; by
Q1; buy nothing of me but F   31 God be wi' you] Q1 (God bwy you); and so God be with you Q3   31 God bless] Q1; God
plesse Q3   35 hussy] Q1 (huswye); huswife F   36 warlike lines] Q1; warlike loynes Q3; wearie limbes F   38 sick. One] Q1;
dead i'th Spittle of a F   40 use . . . of] Q1; something leane to Cut-purse of quick F   42 scars] Q1; cudgelled scarres F   43
swear] Q1; swore F   **Scene 19** 2 And to] Q1; Vnto F   4 stock] Q1; Royalty F   7 we] Q1; you F   8 mightiness] Q1
(mightines); mightinesse Q3   10 rub or bar] Q1; Rub, or what Impediment F

FRENCH KING We have but with a cursenary eye   15
        O'erviewed them. Pleaseth your grace
        To let some of your Council sit with us;
        We shall return our peremptory answer.
KING Go lords, and sit with them,
        And bring us answer back.   20
        Yet leave our cousin Katherine here behind.
FRENCH KING With all our hearts.

> *Exit* FRENCH KING *and the lords* [EXETER *and* BURGUNDY].
> *Manet* KING, KATHERINE, *and the Gentlewoman* [ALICE]

KING Now Kate, you have a blunt wooer here left with you. If I could win thee
        at leapfrog, or with vaulting with my armour on my back into my saddle,
        without brag be it spoken, I'd make compare with any. But leaving that,   25
        Kate, if thou takest me now, thou shalt have me at the worst. And in
        wearing, thou shalt have me better and better. Thou shalt have a face that
        is not worth sun-burning. But dost thou think that thou and I, between St.
        Denis and St. George, shall get a boy that shall go to Constantinople and
        take the great Turk by the beard, ha, Kate?   30
KATE Is it possible dat me sall love de enemy de France?
KING No, Kate, 'tis impossible you should love the enemy of France, for, Kate,
        I love France so well that I'll not leave a village. I'll have it all mine. Then,
        Kate, when France is mine and I am yours, then France is yours and you
        are mine.   35
KATE I cannot tell what is dat.
KING No, Kate? Why, I'll tell it you in French, which will hang upon my
        tongue like a bride on her new-married husband. Let me see, St. Denis be
        my speed. *Quand France est mon.*
KATE Dat is, when France is yours.   40
KING *Et vous êtes à moi.*
KATE And I am to you.
KING *Donc, France êtes à vous.*
KATE Den France sall be mine.
KING *Et je suis à vous.*   45
KATE And you will be to me.
KING Wilt believe me, Kate? 'Tis easier for me to conquer the kingdom than to
        speak so much more French.

15 cursenary] Q1; cursorary Q3; curselarie F   16 O'erviewed them] Q1; O're-glanced the Articles F   18 return our] Q1;
suddenly / Passe our accept and F   22 FRENCH . . . hearts] Q1; *not in* F   22.1 *Exit* FRENCH KING] Q3; *Exit King* Q1; *exeunt
omnes* F   22.2 *Manet* KING] This edn; *Manet,*Hrry Q1   22.2 *and the Gentlewoman*] Q1; *not in* F   23 thee] Q1; a Lady F   25
without brag] Q1; under the correction of bragging F   25 I'd . . . any] Q1; I should quickly leape into a Wife F   30 great
Turk] Q1; Turke F   31 me sall] Q1; I sould F   32 'tis] Q1 (tis); it is Q3   33 not leave] Q1; will not part with F   34 France
is yours] Q1; yours is France F   38 bride] Q1; new-married Wife F   38 new-married husband] Q1; Husbands Necke F   43
Donc] Q1 (Douck)

KATE Ah, your Majesty has false French enough to deceive de best lady in
    France.   50
KING No, faith, Kate, not I. But Kate, in plain terms, do you love me?
KATE I cannot tell.
KING No? Can any of your neighbours tell? I'll ask them. Come, Kate, I know
    you love me. And soon, when you are in your closet, you'll question this
    lady of me. But I pray thee, sweet Kate, use me mercifully, because I love   55
    thee cruelly. That I shall die, Kate, is sure. But for thy love, by the Lord,
    never. What, wench, a straight back will grow crooked, a round eye will
    grow hollow, a great leg will wax small, a curled pate prove bald. But a good
    heart, Kate, is the sun and the moon, and rather the sun and not the moon.
    And therefore, Kate, take me. Take a soldier. Take a soldier, take a king.   60
    Therefore, tell me, Kate, wilt thou have me?
KATE Dat is as please the King my father.
KING Nay, it will please him. Nay, it shall please him, Kate. And upon that
    condition, Kate, I'll kiss you.
KATE *Oh, mon Dieu! Je ne voudrai faire quelque chose pour tout de monde! Ce n'est*   65
    point votre façon en faveur!
KING What says she, lady?
ALICE Dat it is not de fashion en France for de maids, before dey be married,
    to – *ma foi, j'oublie,* what is to *baiser?*
KING To kiss, to kiss. Oh, that 'tis not the fashion in France for the maids to   70
    kiss before they are married.
ALICE *Oui, si votre grace.*
KING Well, we'll break that custom. Therefore, Kate, patience, perforce, and
    yield. Before God, Kate, you have witchcraft in your kisses, and may
    persuade with me more than all the French Council. Your father is   75
    returned.

    Enter the FRENCH KING *and all the Lords* [EXETER *and* BURGUNDY]

        How now, my lords?
FRENCH KING Brother of England, we have o'erread the Articles,
        And have agreed to all that we in schedule had.
EXETER Only he hath not subscribèd this: 80
        Where your Majesty demands
        That the King of France, having any occasion
        To write for matter of grant,
        Shall name your Highness in this form,
        And with this addition in French: 85

49 best lady] Q1; most sage Damoiseil F   51 Kate,] Q1; Kate, prethee tell me Q3   51 do you] Q1; Dost thou Q3   54 you love] Q1; thou louest F   55 lady] Q1; Gentlewoman F   55 use] Q1; mocke F   58 prove] Q1; grow F   62 the . . . father] Q1; de Roy mon pere F   64 condition . . . you] Q1; I kisse your Hand F   64 kiss you] Q1; kisse thee Q3   66 *faveur*] Q2 (fauor); fouor Q1   69 *baiser*] Q1; buisse F   74 kisses] Q1; Lippes F   75–6 Your . . . returned] Q1; Heere comes your Father F   77 How . . . lords?] Q1; *not in* F   78–9] Q1; *not in* F   78 o'erread] Q1 (orered); ordered Q3   80 not] Q1; not yet F   80 subscribed this] Q1; subscribed to this Q2

Nostre trés cher fils, Henry Roi d'Angleterre,
Et heir *de France.* And thus in Latin:
Praeclarissimus filius noster Henricus Rex Angliae,
Et heres Franciae.

FRENCH KING Nor this have we so nicely stood upon,   90
    But you, fair brother, may entreat the same.
KING Why, then let this among the rest
    Have his full course. And withal,
    Your daughter Katherine in marriage.
FRENCH KING This, and what else your Majesty shall crave.   95
    God that disposeth all give you much joy.
KING Why then, fair Katherine,
    Come, give me thy hand.
    Our marriage will we present solemnise,
    And end our hatred by a bond of love.   100
    Then will I swear to Kate, and Kate to me,
    And may our vows, once made, unbroken be.

[Exeunt] Finis

---

90 have . . . upon] Q1; I haue not Brother so deny'd F   91 may entreat . . . same] Q1; shall make me let it passe F   93 full course] Q1; full recourse Q2   95–6] Q1; *not in* F   99 marriage] Q1; matriage Q3   101 will] Q1; shall F   101 Kate to] Q1; you to F   102 vows . . . be] Q1; Oathes well kept and prosp'rous be F   102 be.] Q1; bee? Q2

TEXTUAL NOTES

Scene 1

Act 1 scene 2 in the Folio text.

0 SD *Enter . . .* CLARENCE For the re-naming of Henry's earls, see Introduction, p. 23.

0 SD *Enter . . . Attendants.* Cutting the Prologue and the whole of 1.1 allows the 'two bishops', Canterbury and Ely, to enter here with the other nobles, and makes it unnecessary for Henry to summon them, as he does in F's 1.2.1–3. This suggests that in the staging the Archbishop of Canterbury and the bishop, Ely, were identifiable simply as churchmen from their dress, probably with bishops' mitres on their heads. Only one bishop speaks, and the other may have been no more than a mute escort, if he survived Q's cutting of Ely's part onto the stage at all. F specifies 'the two Bishops' at the beginning of 1.1, and at line 6 of 1.2 (TLN 152).

2 cousin Exeter was Henry's uncle, not his cousin. Westmorland, whose lines Exeter takes over here, was the cousin that Henry addresses in F. In Q Henry correctly addresses Exeter as 'uncle' at line 180.

3 touching Possibly a memory from F's 1.1.79, where the Archbishop says he has to tell the king about causes 'As touching France'. See Introduction, p. 24.

6 Sure Q's 'Shure' is the first clear indication that the text was transmitted aurally at some point. See Introduction, p. 16.

9 my wise and learned lord F has 'My learned Lord' at line 6. Here F has 'my deare and faithfull Lord'.

10 same. Q's punctuation here and elsewhere (lines 13, 28 etc.) observes the pauses more strongly than the grammar. In both of these cases a semi-colon would be more appropriate to the flow of the sentence-structure than a full stop. The stop is retained here because it must be a better reflection of the Q rhythms and the recorder's sense of the speech's flow.

13 to. See line 10n.

15 the sleeping sword F has 'our sleeping Sword', a royal possessive. Otherwise, in this scene Q uses the royal 'we', while F uses the singular.

16 in the name of God Both F and Q use this oath, a mark of the early provenance of both source manuscripts. After the Act of 1606 oaths which named God directly were moderated or cut out.

17 After this conjuration The change of preposition in Q dilutes the force of F's 'Vnder', yet calls attention to its power.

20 in baptism A less focussed preposition than F's 'with', but making the same point, that baptism cleansed the flesh of original sin.

21 BISHOP Q, beginning page 2 (A2v), omits the speech prefix, although the catchword '*Bish.*' does appear on the preceding page.

22 faith A sharp word for a bishop to use here. F's 'selues' is more simply descriptive.

23–4 there . . . France Q's first stumble over the metre; in F, as here, the first four words belong in the previous line, which Q leaves as an emphatic half-line, and the full line has two more syllables. In Q the effect of making line 23 a half-line produces a twelve-syllable line, even in its compressed version of F.

25 Pharamond Q's '*Pharamount*' (later '*Pharamont*') may be a mishearing.

26 female Q omits the Latin in F, which this line glosses, and converts 'woman' into 'female'. The bishop repeats the line at 38, where F's version does use 'Female'.

28 France, See line 10n. Here Q's colon, tantamount to a full stop, seems too heavy, leaving line 29 dangling as a separate sentence without a verb. Lightening the punctuation seems necessary for the grammar.

30 writers Q normalises F's 'Authors', conceivably from a memory of F's 'Writers' in a section cut from between lines 46 and 47.

31 lies Q's word is more emphatic than the neutral F 'is'.

32 Sabeck The Q memory may have conflated 'Sala' and 'Elbe' to make this word. Salic law was given its name from the river called Sala or Salia.

32 Elbe Q's '*Elme*' replaces the exotic name with a more familiar one. F has 'Elue'.

33 Charles the Fifth A copyist's replacement for Charlemagne; Charles the Great in F.

39 as . . . before The bishop does have a prior statement about Salic land being in Meissen in F, immediately after naming the Sala and Elbe rivers. The line was omitted in Q.

45 function i.e., defunction (F), death.

46 Godly supposed See line 16n. Q's word may be a mishearing of F's reading, 'Idly'.

47 Hugh Capet Q here deletes nine lines explaining Pharamond and other historical figures, including Charlemagne. A further two lines linking Capet's usurpation of the line of Charlemagne are also cut.

48 fine F's 'find' may be a compositor's d/e misreading of the original, which Q gives correctly. In the three pages of *Sir Thomas More* by Hand D, thought to be Shakespeare's, the two letters are very similar. The F text has seven other likely d/e misreadings. See NCS *Henry V*, p. 214.

50 the Lady Inger Probably a mishearing of F's 'th'Lady *Lingare*', another likely d/e misreading. Holinshed has 'Lingard'. In F her father is confusingly called '*Charlemaine*', although he was actually Charles II. Possibly to avoid the confusion, Q takes the name of another Charles, named in F as Charlemagne's true heir. Q cuts a further ten lines of names in the lineage after this, picking up again at a reference to '*Charles* the foresaid Duke of Loraine'.

53 King Pepin Not named before in the Q account, but cited in F in the first cut, after line 46.

54 Charles F has '*Lewes*', named in the section of F cut after line 47.

57 Howbeit Confusion over punctuation suggests two alternative readings here: either Q's comma at the end of line 56 makes 'Howbeit' mean 'although', or 'even though', or else it should be a full stop, and means 'However'. The former would make the Archbishop's conclusion into a sentence of fifteen lines. This edition has assumed that each example (41–55) stands as a sentence in itself.

60 **embase** 'imbace', probably meaning 'debase', its sound distinguished from 'bar' two lines earlier. F's 'imbarre' has been variously translated into 'unbar' or 'embar', a reference to heraldic bars which ran crosswise over a shield.

60 **causes** F's 'titles' fits better with the heraldic language of 'embar' here, as Q's word suits an equivalent of 'debase'.

62 **we** Throughout this scene in Q Henry consistently uses the royal 'we', apart from line 15, whereas F equally consistently uses the first person singular.

64 **the Book of Numbers** Holinshed quotes from the fourth Book of Moses in the Old Testament (Bishops' Bible), 'If a man dye, and have no sonne, ye shall turne his inheritance to his daughter'. Q replaces F's 'man' with 'son', presumably by involuntary association with 'daughter'.

66–7 Q's lineation has been retained here, although the F lineation, which puts its equivalent to 'Noble lord' into line 66, and makes the rest of 67 and 68 a single line, is metrically better. Q's lineation, especially in the bishop's speeches, appears to make occasional use of short lines for extra emphasis, as at line 23 and 70.

67 **own . . . flag,** Q's punctuation lets the urgings flow as a sequence of exhortations. A stricter grammar would require each to be a separate sentence. Conceivably the third urging, 'Go, my dread lord', should be a sentence on its own, but Q does not make the distinction, and the flow has been retained here in the punctuation.

69 **claim,** F has another half-line here, completing a ten-syllable line. This may reflect either the use of half-lines for emphasis, or the scribe's forgetfulness.

75 **Foraging** A corruption of F's 'Forrage in', creating a grammatical misuse of an apparently unfamiliar verb.

77 **the full power of France** repeated from line 73. Possibly a sign of the person who was dictating to the scribe using his memory to complement his reading. The F text has 'the full Power of France' for 73, and 'the full pride of France' for 77.

80. Four further speeches of exhortation, a total of 21 lines, from Ely, Exeter, Westmorland and Canterbury, are cut here. One of them is Canterbury's offer to raise for the war 'such a mightie Summe / As never did the Clergie at one time / Bring in to any of your Ancestors.'

85 **coursing sneakers** F's 'coursing snatchers' is the more technical term. When hunting hares the 'snatch' was the capture. Q's word is from F's line 109, where the Scots come 'sneaking'.

88 **Unmasked . . . for** Q's version of this line, unlike F's, obscures the point that Edward left England to conduct his campaign in France.

91–2. Three lines in the F text, amplifications of the story about the Scottish attack, are omitted here.

91 **defences** This plural in Q is the only survivor of five insistent uses of 'defend' or 'defence' in F.

92 **bruit** A distinct change and modification to the F version. F's 'th'ill neighbourhood' is Henry's polite echo of a proverb as a euphemism to signify the dangerous Scots

across its northern border. He is developing his reference to the 'giddy neighbour' ten lines before, which Q cuts. Q's version simply refers to fears of attack.

94 exemplified Q's normalisation of F's 'exampl'd' damages the metre.

98–9 impounded . . . Scots Q is careful to keep F's loaded word. Holinshed's *Chronicle of Scotland* states that Henry IV captured the eight-year-old James I of Scotland in 1406 when he was shipwrecked off Ravenscar in Yorkshire. Technically, the shipwreck meant that he was a 'stray' rather than a prisoner, but the Regent in Scotland was happy to have him kept out of the country. Keeping a 'stray' usually referred to the impounding of a wandering cow. Young King James I was kept at the English court for several years, and followed Henry V to fight alongside him in France in 1420, when the Scots sent an army of 7,000 men there to fight for the Dauphin against the English. Shakespeare knew Holinshed's history of Scotland as well as his account of Henry's reign in the English chronicle.

100 caitiff Not a word used in F, it suggests contempt as well as captivity. The intrusive phrase breaks up the metre, which runs regularly in F, breaking at 'Stray', and making a complete line up to 'France' without the four-syllable intrusion of 'like a caitiff'.

104 LORD Q's failure to name this speaker suggests that the original staging allocated it to an anonymous lord, certainly not to one of the two clergymen present. Ely was unlikely to contradict his superior. F's speech-heading, which in this section generally distinguishes '*Bish.Ely.*' from '*Bish.Can.*', gives it to Ely, where Holinshed specified Westmorland.

108 To his F makes the eagle England a mother. Q starts by thinking of the eagle as male, then follows F by reverting to it as a mother in the next line.

110 spoil Q changes the incomprehensible F word 'tame', aphetic from 'attame', to break in, into something more manageable.

111 EXETER This is Exeter's first speech in Q, after his opening question. In F he has already spoken twice.

112 cursed F's 'crush'd' seems appropriately less emphatic here.

113 traps Q solves the metrical problem created by its conflation of two F lines by cutting out F's wordplay of 'pretty . . . petty'.

115 controls Q's paraphrase falsifies F's metre.

117 Congrueth Q's case-change of F's verb allows it to retain the term while normalising it, and adjusting into a simpler one-line metre.

118 True; The bishop's extra word in Q damages the metre, and sets up one ten-syllable and one twelve-syllable line. It interrupts the smooth flow with which Canterbury picks up Exeter's argument.

119 fate Q's word may be a mishearing of F's 'state'.

120 added Q normalises the F image, which is of an archery target being fixed onto a moving object.

121 awe Q offers a neat monosyllable which by providing a synonym for F's 'rule in nature' manages to keep the metre. The word is taken from its original use in F at line 153.

123 sort Q's singular offers a similar meaning to F's plural. A 'sort' was a rank or category.

130 behold The plural verb falsifies the grammar.

132–3 Q omits a couplet about the 'poore Mechanicke Porters' with their heavy burdens.

132 lading Q's word is more apt for honey than F's .

134 caning Q's adjective, 'caning', is a distinctive usage here. F's 'yawning' is a straightforward term which the Q word must paraphrase. It is possible that the word was meant to be 'cunning', which in Elizabethan writing would be easily misread since it has nine exactly similar minim downstrokes between the c and the g. The chief justification for seeing such a word is that it picks up the idea of justice, heavily exercised on idlers who work as coney or 'cunny'-catchers, a term not infrequently associated with 'conning' or 'cunning'. But a much more likely if portentous reading would keep 'caning', which was retained in Q3, as a real if obsolete word. Used in the fifteenth and sixteenth centuries (OED v.2), it meant the scum or dross formed in mis-brewed ale that has gone sour. If it was meant to be such an unusual term, and F's the more normal alternative, its rarity would relate it to 'leno' at 13.11, Q's exotic choice in place of F's 'pander'. 'Leno' has suggested to some editors that the Q text might show signs of a Shakespearean input.

136 May . . . moment A version of F's 'End in one purpose' (echoed incorrectly at 142), used here in place of F's 'work contrariously'.

138 several Q repeats a word from the previous line to repair the metre, knocked askew by the omission of a phrase and by a twelve-syllable line in F.

139 one self sea Possibly the convention of the 'self-' prefix as an intensifier, like 'self-same', was prompted by a memory of the word lost at 1.22, used here to replace F's simpler noun-adjective.

143 defect Q's word fits the context rather better than F's more portentous 'defeat'.

149 beaten Q's word loses F's continuation of the dog imagery, where dogs get their teeth into their quarry and 'worry' it.

151 the messenger . . . the Dauphin F's plural 'Messengers' is made singular here, although the stage direction at line 157 suggests at least two men. They would comprise one ambassador followed by his servant. Q normalises F.

153 our awe See note to line 121.

151–8 Three short lines and one of twelve syllables in this eight-line speech indicate text omitted. F has twelve lines by the king, from which these are taken in a fairly rough paraphrase. Q omits the idea of the silent grave as the alternative to chronicling their deeds.

157 like tongueless mutes F's line speaks of a Turkish mute with tongueless mouth.

158 a paper epitaph F's 'waxen' epitaph is taken over in Q by the reference to 'chronicles' (F 'history').

157.1 *the Ambassadors* See note to line 151.

158 the Dauphin's Q omits Henry's innuendo, in calling the Dauphin 'Cosin', that he has a claim to the French crown through his lineage.

159 coming In F's word 'greeting' Henry is rather more formal, inviting the ambassador to speak his initial courtesies.

162 I Q allows the single ambassador the singular pronoun, although he has, as in F, used plurals in the previous line. Q specifies the entry of plural ambassadors at 1.157.1, as does F.

163 pleasure A delicate word, suggesting some embarrassment at the sneer he is about to unveil. F's 'meaning' is far more neutral.

165 spirit Q moderates F's 'passion', reducing the force of the implication that Henry can control his rage.

167 boldness Q implies a need for courage in the messenger, not the plain speaking which the F Henry asks for.

169 in fine F's 'in few' takes up Henry's invitation to speak bluntly. Q's word instead proposes a brief summary.

172–4 Two lines in F are compressed into the first phrase here, which Q gave a line to itself. The following two lines lost their metre, and have been corrected here.

178 crave Q's word shows more contempt than F's 'claime'.

181 message . . . present Q's line reverses F's nouns, substitutes the neutral 'message' for F's mildly sarcastic 'paines', and paraphrases the rest.

183 will . . . God's Q omits a short phrase, throwing the scansion out, but adding 'such' to bring it back.

187–9 With chases . . . them. Q loses the rhythm for three lines by putting 'with chases' at the end of line 186, giving the next two twelve and fourteen syllables respectively.

191–2 Q skips a phrase from F in 191, and compresses three lines into two at the cost of giving line 192 two extra feet.

191 our self F's text is surely correct here. Q's 'our selues' confuses the royal plural with the national.

193 we . . . our F has 'I' and 'my', which here makes it more emphatically the response of the king in person to the Dauphin's jeer, rather than an official statement. The same change of person recurs at 195 and 196.

195 our Q's omission is a compositor slip, since the scansion and grammar both require it. The compositor slipped again in 197.

197 like Q's 'lide' was probably a wrong fount error.

198 full a Q's scribe or dictator replaced the original with the conventional 'full of glory'.

199 we Q's consistent use of the plural here moves towards a collective, embracing all the attending English lords in his claim. F's use of the singular here and at 209–11 below lays stress on the personal nature of the quarrel between Henry and the Dauphin. It may be that Q's elimination of the Dauphin from Agincourt was a consideration in shifting the personal 'I' here into the national 'we'.

201–2 Again, Q compresses three lines into two by substituting a monosyllable 'him' for F's 'the pleasant Prince', with the result that one line has twelve syllables and the next fourteen, as at 186–7.

203 fly . . . them Q blurs F's image of the cannon balls carrying vengeance.

206 Aye, Q1 intensifies F's addition, which may be an error. A sharp concluding pair of lines seems necessary here.

208–10 In an otherwise accurate version of F's scansion, Q here compresses three lines of F into two. This text re-lines as in F.

215 See . . . hence. Q's phrase is more curtly dismissive than F's 'Fare you well'. It also instructs the English lords to do the courtesies of escorting the ambassador and his servant offstage, while Henry turns to the business of the war. Its urgency may be reflected in the shortening of Henry's last speech, cutting six of F's twelve lines.

218 collection The Q recorder's memory conflates F's 'proportions . . . collected' into 'collection', which calls for some adjustment to the grammar.

218–20 Q's cuts in this speech led to lines at the end of the cut being compressed, with the loss of a rhyme. Q's version of Henry's speech still ends with a rhyming couplet, but loses the first of F's pair. The first has been restored by re-lineation here.

Scene 2
Act 2 scene 1 in the NCS text.

0 NIM *and* BARDOLPH F's Chorus intervening between Q's scenes 1 and 2 allows time for the Eastcheap group to change before reappearing in this scene. See Introduction, p. 11. F's specification of Nim and Bardolph's military titles for the entry to open this scene, which may indicate an authorial expectation of what they would have worn, is ignored by Q, which does however keep the specification of their new titles in the text.

1 Good morrow Q makes both entrants offer the same greeting, which F varies with an initial 'Well met'. The fact that they greet each other probably means they enter from separate doors.

3 is . . . thee Q makes F's rather formal plural into a singular, creating a grammatical solecism by converting 'are' into 'is'.

6–7 and there's . . . it In Q Nim introduces his catchphrase at the end of his second speech in the scene, at the earliest possible moment. F gives it to him only at his eighth, line 35 here.

8 Bardolph's speech begins with an inversion from F, the two exchanges at lines 13–17 and 8–12 being transposed.

10 mare Q's word, concluding one of Nim's proverbial sayings, is altogether more fitting than F's , which may be a misreading of Q's word in the F manuscript.

12 and there . . . it Q renews Nim's catchphrase. See note to lines 6–7.

14 What a . . . throats? Transposed from a later intervention by Bardolph at line 57.

18 Goodmorrow . . . Here . . . Pistol Q's repetition may either be a false start by the reviser, or an initial welcome to Pistol, and then in warning to Nim. If the latter, the initial greeting is an addition to F.

19 be quiet The Q form is a direct request to keep silent. F's version is a softer plea to keep under control.

20 NIM Q supplies a speech prefix omitted in F. F sets the ironic greeting at the end of

Bardolph's speech, which does not fit his peace-making attempts, or Pistol's fury against Nim.

21 Pistol's heavily iambic lines are usually converted into verse from F's prose. Q sets it uncertainly as verse, as it characteristically does with all the prose scenes. Here it has been returned to prose. See Introduction, p. 20, and Appendix 2.

21 slave Q's term appears to lose one of Pistol's many insults by reference to different sorts of dog. Since editors have proposed alternatives to the word 'Tyke' used by F, Q's choice may just be a simplification of a too-rarely used word. The word 'slave' probably came from Pistol's other line at 59.

21 by gad's lugs F's 'by this hand' is much milder, certainly not a blasphemous oath. Since the copy for both texts preceded the 1606 Act against blasphemy on stage, either Q's player or reviser must have chosen to intensify the phrase here.

23 half a score Q reduces the number from F's twelve or fourteen.

25 Corporal The Hostess's use of the military title suggests that its joke value was lost to the revisers. The Hostess uses the full name twice, here and in the next line, but not in F.

25 Nim Hardly a possessive in Q, and not used in F, Q's plural may be a copyist's error.

26 committed! . . . Good Q omits Bardolph's plea for peace, and tacks the Hostess's next line onto the end of her previous speech, making the brief intervening exchange between Nim and Pistol part of their longer exchange following.

28 Push Q's adaptation of F's more common expression 'Pish' may reflect Nim's distinctive pronunciation, but it was more likely voiced with the different vowel in performance so as to give Pistol occasion to take up the word in his response. It is not used in F except in a different context (see note to line 61).

30 shog off? In F this impolite request is addressed to the Hostess, who has spoken last. Q's switch in lines 26–7 now addresses it to Pistol, making a nonsense of his statement, since he now says that he wants Pistol to leave and also that he wants to speak to him alone.

30 *solus* The Q copyist evidently understood the word better than Pistol is supposed to. This edition italicises the word as Nim uses it, as a theatrical term, but keeps it in roman for Pistol's use, to differentiate the meanings the two men give it.

32 messful A markedly more colourful term than F's 'nastie'. Conceivably it was the player's own substitution.

33 talk F's 'take' means catch fire, anticipating the metaphor of Pistol as a gun which follows. Q misses the play on the word, and normalises.

33–4 flashing . . . cock Q emphasises the metaphor's tenor rather than its vehicle. F's version, 'take . . . cocke . . . fire will follow', refers to the firing-sequence. Q bypasses the allusion to the cocking-piece of a pistol, which enables the weapon to be fired, in favour of the allusion to Pistol's penis.

35 humour, Pistol Q transposes the name from F's position after 'fowle with me'.

36 An Q's 'And' is a common version of an = if.

40 groaning Q normalises F's 'doting', which is chiefly useful in F for its alliteration.

40.1 *They draw* F has no stage directions to say when Nim and Pistol draw and then sheathe their swords. From the dialogue, it seems that they should draw first at line 25, as the Hostess's exclamation suggests. In F they would sheathe them when Bardolph intervenes, but his line is cut in Q. The first appearance of the direction to draw here indicates that in the Q version their first flourish was here and not at line 25. But neither text states when they should sheathe their swords, which would probably come when Bardolph intervenes again and Pistol says 'fury shall abate', at line 43, so Q may be nearly as deficient as F in marking such stage directions.

41 kill him Bardolph's interposition is made blunter and rather less colourful in Q.

43 abate Q cuts Pistol's offer of his hand to Nim, which would require them first to sheathe their swords.

44 your In Q Nim consistently uses the second-person plural, whereas Pistol always uses the singular. F gives Nim a single 'thy' to Pistol in this line, which Q makes plural.

46 'Couple gorge' A phrase that might prompt Pistol to draw his sword again. Q has no stage direction for it here, however, unlike lines 40 and 61.

46 thee defy Q's inversion makes F's look like a compositor's normalisation.

46 A . . . hound Q paraphrases here, keeping the imagery of dogs.

47 No . . . infamy! Compressed in Q from twenty words to seven.

49 Quickly The Q text does not capitalise this word, an obvious copyist's error.

49 *Paco!* Q approximates F's Latin *pauca*, short for *pauca verba*, in few words.

50 there . . . enough. F's 'there's enough to go to' does not make good sense. Rowe proposed 'there's enough. Go to', which most editions have adopted. Q's trimmer version is a good alternative.

50.1 *the BOY* Depending on what was in the transcriber's mind, Q's use of 'the' may signify either a specific boy player who was Falstaff's 'boy' in *2 Henry IV*, or the specific boy player who served in the company for this play.

51 Hostess In F the Boy puts the plea to Pistol, calling him 'Mine Hoast', like Nim. He makes no mention of Falstaff being sick, which F emphasises, saying that he 'would to bed'. The remaining section of his speech in Q takes his being in bed for granted.

51 you, Host Pistol Q reverses F's addressees in making the plea.

54 days. Q cuts F's additional phrase, 'The King has kild his heart', along with the later references by Pistol and Nim (after line 73).

55 Q omits any exit for the Hostess and the Boy, although the Hostess returns at line 71, and the Boy has no further lines. They must exit here, since Bardolph sets about reconciling Nim and Pistol.

56 Pistol . . . Nim Bardolph adds their names in Q, as if, improbable though it must be, to ensure the audience knows the identity of those remaining after the exit.

57 be enemies Bardolph paraphrases in Q. F's reference to keeping knives at each other's throats, installed at line 13 in Q, was taken from here.

61 compound In a phrase cut from Q, F here uses the word 'push' that Pistol deploys in Q at line 28.

61.1 *They draw* Unlike the previous occasions, F has the stage direction here. Neither text, however, indicates when they sheathe their swords again.

62 by . . . sword Nothing in either text signals that Bardolph draws as well, but this oath suggests that he should. F puts it at the beginning of the speech, Q, less emphatically, at the end.

64 Q cuts Bardolph's second intervention between the contestants here. The lines omitted end in F's 'prethee put vp', which should signal the sheathing of their swords.

64 I shall . . . betting? Unlike F, Q repeats the exact phrasing of the first request, line 58.

65 ready Q substitutes a near-synonym for F's 'present'. Both imply immediate payment.

66 combine Q's 'combind' is most likely a copyist's d/e misreading. It is also in Q2 and Q3, however, and possibly its survival into the latter text, more thoughtfully edited than Q2, indicates that 'combind' had some currency as a word on its own, as an intensive form of 'bind'.

66 as Q's word is stronger than F's 'and'.

68 accrue Q's 'occrue' suggests the copyist had an imperfect command of the word.

72 came of men F's 'come of women' is the proverbial phrase. The Hostess's speech is curtailed in Q, and three of the last four exchanges between Pistol and Nim are cut, as if the peace between them was thought to be the scene's real conclusion, with only the briefest news about Falstaff remaining to be delivered.

73 tertian contagian F's 'burning quotidian Tertian' is reduced, and the 'lamentable' sight becomes merely 'wonderful'. Pistol and Nim's identification of it as a result of the king's turning him away are cut, like the earlier reference (line 54n).

73 Q cuts an exchange of three short speeches between Nim and Pistol in F about the king having, in Pistol's words, left Falstaff's heart 'fracted and corroborate'.

Scene 3

Act 2 scene 2 in the NCS text.

0.1 GLOSTER Q replaces F's 'Bedford' with Gloster throughout. This edition retains the original spelling, which reflects the pronunciation then and now.

1 too bold Q, which has already lost F's metre with its intrusive address 'my lord', makes the verse into prose by normalising the F version of the adjective.

2 Three lines from Westmorland are cut here in Q, along with the elimination of the rest of his part. Gloster (lines 3–6) takes a speech from Exeter.

4 graced F's 'dull'd and cloy'd' as a doublet is replaced in Q by a more familiar pair, the replacement word picked up from line 1.

5 to sell Q normalises the intensive 'so sell' in F.

7 Q adds a line to identify the particular villain Gloster has been speaking of. The extra line was made necessary by the switch of Exeter's speech (lines 3–6) to Gloster. See Introduction, pp. 26–7.

8 sirs . . . fair A Q misreading of F's manuscript 'sits' and its singular 'winde'. Q consequently needs to turn 'winde' into the verbal form. Q also adds the formal mode of direct address to line 1.

9 **my lord of** By repeating the words applied to Cambridge, Q loses the sarcasm of F's 'my kinde Lord' for Masham.

11–12 **power** Q's singular is justified by the change from F's plural in the next line.

12 **Will . . . France?** Q paraphrases three lines of F.

13 MASHAM This edition retains the naming preferred by Q.

14–16 Q cuts Henry's five-line response to Masham, shortens Cambridge's four-line speech to one (actually a line and a half, but set as one), and reduces Gray's three lines to two.

16 **for your sake** Q abbreviates to a more ambiguous version of F's effusive 'hearts create of duty, and of zeale'.

19 **than reward** Q, by omitting F's 'quittance of', loses the decasyllabic rhythm.

21 **shine** Q replaces F's 'toyle' with a more alliterative and less contrastive word.

23 **service** Q's singular normalises, but loses the metre.

24–6 Q omits the initial phrase which answers Masham, and turns Henry directly to speak to Exeter. The omission helps to reduce his five lines to four, breaking the lines at the caesura and adding a few extra syllables to lines 25 and 26.

29–30 Q stumbles over the transcription, enlarging F's 'example' and omitting 'by his sufferance' from the next line, damaging the metre as a result.

34 **his** Q normalises F's intensifying 'much'.

36 **the** Q reduces the force of F's 'this'.

37–41 Q's five lines misline F's six drastically. This edition restores the F lineation.

41–2 **and the . . . loves** Q adds a phrase with the gist of the F meaning.

41 **and the rest** Q consistently eliminates Scrope's name, the one used in F in the text and for speech headings, in favour of 'Masham'. Here Q avoids using any names other than Cambridge's.

42 **state** Q's replacement for F's 'person' here is like its shift elsewhere of Henry's first-person pronouns from singular to plural, transferring priority from the person to the nation.

44–5 Q, misunderstanding the half-line linkage in the metre, gives Cambridge one long line.

44 **Me** Q's pronoun is grammatically less correct than F's , possibly by a memory of the 'me' in the next line, or the repetitions by Masham and Gray at line 46.

46 **Sovereign** Titles seem to have been interchangeable, in both F and Q. Here Q uses a word that appears in the next line of F, but is cut from Q.

49 Q's long line comes from a slight muddle over the formal naming of Masham and Gray.

50–1 **we . . . I** Q reverses F's pronouns.

51 Q cuts the name of Westmorland.

52 **why change . . . colour?** Q paraphrases, cutting Henry's twelve words to four.

53 **What . . . papers** Q takes a phrase out of F's line 52, and links it directly to line 54, which is in both texts.

54 **hath** Q's singular is a more straightforward use than F's plural.

56 MASHAM F gives this speech to Gray as well as Masham. While in F it stands as an unmetrical half-line, Q's trimming of the previous lines makes it perfectly regular.

57 quick The F word is surely correct here, since it opposes 'killed' (F's word for Q's 'done'). Q's word may be a misreading of F's 'quick', or it may be an anticipation of 'quit' at 3.91.

58 reasons Q's word is transposed from line 60, where F's 'reasons' is made 'conscience'.

58 forestalled and done A stock doublet, replacing F's more forceful 'supprest and kill'd', which refers more directly to the conspirators' former arguments.

59 ask for Although neither Q nor F supplies a stage direction, the likelihood is that all three conspirators kneel for mercy at lines 55–6. If so, Q's term here is more direct than F's 'talke of'.

60 conscience turn Q changes F's 'reasons', possibly because the F term has already been used at line 58. Strictly, 'conscience' should be a plural, since in modern usage every person's conscience is personal. Here the collective sense is unlikely, since Q keeps the plural verb. Perhaps the extra syllable required to make the plural sound 'consciences' was elided in speech.

60 upon i.e., like a knife. Q's substitution may be a memory of 'upon' in the next line. F's 'into' has the more mental or spiritual application.

61 them Henry's simile plays on the double meaning of 'worry' as being caught by hounds and as the guilty conscience which produces the 'shame' of line 59. F's 'you' is more personal than Q's pronoun, which refers to the simile's 'masters'.

64 to . . . him Q's 'grace', from line 4, concentrates this paraphrase of one and a half lines in F.

64–7 Q reduces F's five lines to four.

66 vile Q's 'vilde', or vild, was an alternative spelling for the modern term. Conceivably, without the compositor's terminal 'e', it may have been one of the instances of d/e misreadings of the original text.

71 false man Q replaces F's name, 'Lord *Scroope*' here, because it is not otherwise used in the Q text. It has already identified his name as the lord of Masham with its insertion of line 7.

73 counsel A neutral alternative to F's plural, also used at line 58 in F, although the Q word carries some implication about the king's official 'Council' of advisers.

74 secrets . . . heart A slightly more conventional and less emphatic substitution for F's 'bottome of my soule', Q's phrase does carry a rather heavier sense of intimacy.

77–80 Q paraphrases these lines, before cutting the next 38 lines from Henry's speech.

80 from Maxwell's conjecture, emending the Q and F alternatives, has its appeal. Q however is not so obviously a wrong version of the image that it justifies a change.

81–2 Q compresses the last two and a half lines of Henry's speech in F into two lines. Line 81 starts with the F half-line, making one of fourteen syllables.

83–5 The Q compositor, and most likely the scribe who wrote the copy, set these three speeches giving each one two lines, making six in all. They have no verse metre, and read as formal prose.

84–5 Lord of Masham Exeter, if a Q reviser, here as before cuts out F's extra name '*Scroope*'.

89 Q preserves the metre, despite the shift from 'Highness' to 'Majesty', by cutting out a redundant preposition.

90 After Masham's speech, which is identical in F and Q, Q cuts both of the equivalent speeches by Cambridge (six lines) and Gray (four).

93 **proclaimed and fixed** Both Q's line and F's shorter version have too many syllables. The main error is likely to be Q's , since on most occasions when a cut is made Q's version of the preceding lines stumbles. Here an extra phrase in Q, 'and fixed', which makes a doublet, throws the metre of the next line out. The next four lines following in F are cut.

95 **redress** A more objective word than F's 'reuenge'.

97–102 Q mislines, while keeping the F words almost exactly. The lineation has been corrected here.

102 **deeds amiss** Q makes an indifferent substitution for F's 'deare offences', which scans rather better.

102.1 *Exit . . . lords* Taylor (*Three Studies*, p. 73), attempting to calculate how Q might have been performed by only eleven actors, points out that there is no sign in Q that the three conspirators were escorted offstage.

104 **successively** An awkward paraphrase in Q of F's unusual wording 'like glorious'.

105–7 The last three lines of the scene in Q summarise 10 lines in F. Line 105 is from the first two of the cut lines, and the final rhyming couplet is given exactly.

Scene 4
Act 2 scene 3 in the NCS text.

0.1 *a* BOY Q's use of the indefinite article is odd, since the play has only the one boy, who has already appeared in Scene 2. It may reflect uncertain casting at the time the Q text was being put together.

1 **sweetheart** Q's word is markedly more ordinary than F's 'honey sweet husband'.

2 **No fur** An incomprehensible Pistolism. F's line begins 'No: for . . . ', but that has no direct relation to Pistol's negation. Conceivably it is a Pistolian way of saying 'No further'. It is unlikely to be the modern 'no fear', which did not become current until the end of the nineteenth century. Julius Caesar's use of 'no fear' at 2.1.190 to the Soothsayer means the opposite of the modern usage. Pistol is certainly resisting his wife's request to accompany him through the first section of the journey to Southampton. This is Pistol's shortest speech in the play, replacing F's thirty words about Falstaff's death, a much briefer statement about which Q gives to Bardolph.

3 **Well . . . him** In the absence of Pistol's lines about the death, a new text is invented for Bardolph.

4 **Aye** In F the Hostess starts by denying Bardolph's thought that Falstaff might be in hell, which Q cuts. The rest of her speech is well presented, apart from a few cuts, including the reference to green fields, and one transposition.

7 **talk of flowers** Q's version of F's most famous crux, which has Falstaff babbling of green fields, is slightly misplaced in Q, but it does allude to a state of mind not unlike Theobald's famous conjectured emendation of F.

12 **upward** F's peculiar 'vp-peer'd' is normalised in Q.

14 on Q's 'on' and F's 'of' mean the same thing, 'against'.

15 he Q consistently uses the less colloquial pronoun instead of F's 'a' throughout this scene, although the F usage does occur in later scenes of the Q text.

16 BOY F gives this line to Bardolph.

20 NIM F gives its version of this line to the Boy.

24 hell fire Q adds a little to F's 'Hell'.

25 God . . . him Bardolph's conventional pietism replaces a joke in F.

26 shog off Q extends F's monosyllable, recalling its previous use at 2.30.

27–30 Q paraphrases Pistol's speech in F, repositioning some colourful phrases, and cutting the exhortation to go to France like leeches to suck blood, and the Boy's response to it. His last sentence follows the Boy's aside in F. Q sets it as verse, but the entire scene is in verse. See Introduction, p. 20.

29 Cophetua It is neatly wrong for Pistol to invoke Cophetua, the king who loved a virtuous dairy-maid, cited by Mercutio in *Romeo and Juliet* 2.1, rather than use the foreign word for care that F gives him.

30 lips F's 'mouth' is a more neutral synonym than Q's word. In F Pistol uses 'Lippes' to the Hostess at the beginning of his speech.

33 Another addition, probably by the player. F's version has less application to the game of kissing and non-kissing just completed. A 'bugle bow' was technically a child's bow made of a sheep's or goat's horn, a horn bow. Its resemblance to the human mouth made it a synonym both for the mouth and for the vagina. See the entry for 'buggle boe' in Williams. Taylor identifies it as a 'buggle-boo', or goblin, taking Pistol to be urging his new wife to 'restrain your wandering spirit' (*Three Studies*, p. 149).

Scene 5
Act 2 scene 4 in the NCS text.

1–3 Q trims F's fourteen-line speech to three, and transfers Exeter's warning at the end of the scene in F to the French King's third line here. The King names three of the four French lords from F, but ignores the Dauphin.

3 In F Exeter delivers this line as his parting shot, a warning to the French king to make haste.

4 My . . . Lord The Dauphin's address to his father is normalised from F, where he specifically calls him father. This loses Q one possible means of identifying him, until the Constable intervenes in response at line 14.

4–5 we . . . arm us Q cuts six lines from this speech, as usual mangling the preceding two lines in the process. The cut leaves line 5 as a half-line, and makes two consecutive lines begin with 'And'.

6 weak and sickly Another varied doublet, for F's 'sick and feeble'.

7 But Q's cut of six lines takes out the first argument, which in F begins 'But', and replaces the 'And' beginning the second argument with the proper conjunction for the first.

9–10 Q's metre is not quite right. It takes 'England' from the previous line in F, leaving it a little short, and uses it in place of F's cut adjective 'Whitsun' to get lines 9 and 10 metrically correct.

12 **So guided by** Again, Q gets the metre right, putting a verb in for F's run of adjectives, 'By a vaine giddie . . . '

14 The constable's first half-line in F completes the Dauphin's last half-line. In Q his next full line from F is compressed to the half-line, 'you deceive yourself', to make one full line, which is metrically perfect, while leaving the Dauphin's last half-line dangling.

15 **ambassador** Q's change from F's plural may reflect the actual staging, where the French ambasaador in scene 1 was not accompanied by any attendant on stage. That was not proper decorum, and the reference here may simply ignore his servant. The singulars in Q's next line indicate the latter.

16 **regard** Q's word may have been derived from the opening scene of F, not used in Q, where Canterbury says that the king is full of 'grace, and faire regard' (TLN 61–2).

17 **agéd** A pointed substitution for F's 'Noble', given that the Dauphin called Henry a 'Youth'.

18–19 As before, the line in Q preceding a long cut from the F text is altered. F has another seven lines by the Constable and an eight-line reply from the Dauphin, here cut to line 18's version of 'How terrible in constant resolution', to which is added, with perfect metre, the wholly invented line 19.

20 **Well,** Q adds this to make up for the long cut before it, and the final half-line. The king repeats the simple 'Harry' from the invented line before, instead of F's 'King *Harry*', which would have helped the metre.

21 The king changes his distanced exhortation to the French princes in F as 'you', to a present-tense statement of what all the French are doing to 'prevent' or stop the English. His fifteen-line speech that follows in F, with its reference to Crécy matching Canterbury's in the first scene, is cut entirely. His brevity here makes him more resolute and commanding than in F.

22 **CONSTABLE** F's messenger is subsumed into the onstage French lord, an economy with slightly awkward consequences, since it makes Exeter march in without any formal announcement. Possibly that was intended.

23 **Bid . . . in** The king's concise phrase, contrasting with F's 'Weele giue them present audience. / Goe, and bring them', suits the loss of ceremony in Q's version of Exeter's entry. It is possible that the change may have been made to economise on attendants.

25 The Dauphin's first line in Q makes up for five in F, developing the recurrent imagery of the English as dogs, here 'coward dogs'.

31 **That borrowed title** Exeter substitutes the noun from Canterbury's 'Salic Law' speech in scene 1, in place of F's 'The borrowed Glories'. He uses it again at line 34, for F's 'wide-stretched Honors'.

34 Q omits a line that is no more than a parenthetical amplification of the three preceding.

37 **old** An almost indifferent variant for F's 'long-vanisht'.

38 **rack't** Q's 'rackte' may be a misreading of F's 'rakt'.

39 **these . . . lines** Q's plural normalises F's distinctive but idiosyncratic pun about the contents of a scroll containing his master's royal lineage.

40 demonstrated Q normalises into a verb F's 'demonstratiue'.

43 famed and famous The Q reviser misunderstands F's superlative 'famed of famous'.

47 In Q the French king's reply seems a little more timorous than F's 'Or else what followes?' It counters the concision of his earlier speeches, the result of Q's cutting.

52–6 Q trims F's eight lines to five, slightly affecting the first and last lines of the cut, and leaving a half-line. The cut eliminates a reference to 'the Bowels of the Lord', and war as a hungry dog.

56 distresséd F's 'betrothed', as an adjective for 'Louers', seems less pointed than Q's word, although the F term may be indicating that the loss of men formally betrothed is heavier than any romantic attachments.

60 we Exeter adopts the formality of Henry in the changes from 'we' to 'I' of the first scene. Conceivably as a transcriber he was responsible for that scene's plurals.

60 greeting too This may be a reviser's misreading of the F text, which has 'to', a legitimate though rare doubling of the preposition for emphasis. Q's version is a little more commonplace. It has its own point, since Exeter began by presenting Henry's greeting to the king, and can now add those to the Dauphin.

61 In F the French king gives a temporising reply before the Dauphin is allowed to respond. Q removes his reply to later, and brings the Dauphin straight in to pick up Exeter's invitation.

62 hear Q's word may be a mishearing of F's 'him'. If so, it indicates that the Exeter reviser was speaking his lines to a scribe.

66 Unless The Q reviser repeats his word from line 59, in place of F's 'and if'.

67 Q cuts an entire line here, F's 'Doe not,in graunt of all demands at large'. The cut has no effect on the grammar.

69 wombly vaults F's 'Wombie Vaultages' may have given the reviser a little trouble here. The intrusive 'l' destroys the meaning, and trimming the second word damages the metre. The phrase hints at France's wine-vaults, and at children dying because of the war.

72 Say that The Dauphin's offer of a conjecture in Q is no softer than F's 'Say: if'. Q's unpunctuated words are sharper than F's, and signal his readiness to dissent from what his father may choose to deliver in reply.

72–6 The Dauphin's reply in Q is breathless, one sentence punctuated only with commas (although Q uses a full point and a colon). Nearing the end of his page on C2, the Q compositor stretched his copy to use more space, making lines 73 and 74 into three half-lines. See Appendix 1.

75 according to his youth The Q reviser trimmed F's 'as matching to his Youth and Vanitie', probably to keep the metre, which was thrown out by the intrusive 'so much' at line 74.

81 Between . . . now The reviser lost F's 'the promise of his greener', which lost him the metre, and left him ending in a half-line. Q's 'younger' for F's 'greener' is a routine substitution, normal towards the end of a section. The same memory slip may have generated Q's 'musters' for F 'masters', though that might equally be a mishearing.

85–6 The French king closes the scene not with his three lines at the end in F but with a rough paraphrase of what F gives him to say before the Dauphin responds at line 72.

Scene 6
Act 3 scene 2 in the NCS edition.

0.1 Entry of the Eastcheap group after the French scene with Exeter admits a fresh group of players. Q omits not only the Chorus to Act 3 but the entire first scene of Henry's exhortation to his troops at Harfleur, the famous 'Once more vnto the Breach, Dear friends.' It also omits the extraordinary stage direction calling for '*Scaling Ladders at Harflew*' (see Introduction, p. 22), and Jamy and McMorris to augment the English and Welsh captains. The absence of exit directions suggests that the Q revisers thought of the entire section up to the surrender as one scene.

1 hot service Bardolph's exhortation to charge in F is cut, a logical consequence of cutting Henry's speech before it. Instead, Nim starts the scene in paraphrase, picking up the word 'hot' from the F text, and summarising the rest of his opening speech in the invented word 'service', a military service with which he is not familiar. Every speech in this section is shortened, and all Pistol's and the Boy's songs are cut.

3 die Pistol's last word here rhymes with the last word of his other speech, the only remnant of the songs he sings in F. This line, from 'blows' to 'die', and the last nine words of line 5 are in ballad metre, so have been lined up here roughly as verse.

4 honour In this second speech, not in F, Nim again adds another invented word to his familiar catchphrase.

5 ale The Boy's line is a close paraphrase of F, losing only the last two words, 'and safetie'.

7.1 *beats them in* No exit is given for Llewellyn below, and after the Eastcheap people flee at the end of the Boy's soliloquy Gower enters and addresses him. The position of the exit for Nim, Bardolph and Pistol at line 15 suggests that they and Llewellyn continue to run about onstage while he tries to 'beat them in'; the Boy avoids that fracas to speak his soliloquy, and that after they all escape Llewellyn stays onstage for his meeting with Gower. Envisaging the action in this form entails making no changes to the Q stage directions. What it does require is five lines of knockabout, against the noise of which the Boy speaks.

8 God's plut An addition in Q, the spelling of this exclamation marks Llewellyn as Welsh. His other plosive in this line, 'breaches', is spelt without the unvoiced 'p' sound (F 'breach') in both texts.

10 NIM In F these words are Pistol's, and their shape is much more Pistol's than Nim's. Possibly Q gave them to him to free Pistol, who has to deal with Llewellyn in later scenes. Conceivably Pistol was to hide behind a post, and slip away while Llewellyn was chasing Nim and Bardolph.

11–15 The Boy's soliloquy to the audience is cut in Q from F's 258 words to 68. There is one transposition, of the familiarity with men's pockets joke. The joke about

Pistol's 'killing Tongue' and 'quiet Sword' is cut while the two about Nim's and Bardolph's stealing remain.

15.1 *Exit* . . . BOY See note to line 7 SD. If Llewellyn remains onstage during the Boy's speech, he must spend the time chasing Pistol, Bardolph and Nim around the stage, finally seeing them off at one door, while the Boy slips out by the other. He can then turn back to the centre of the stage, while Gower enters by the door the Boy escaped through.

18 Look you Llewellyn's Welsh was evident in his first plosive in Q, 'Godes plut' at line 8. Here he introduces his most frequently-used catchphrase in both texts. The full speech paraphrases the more ornate F speech adequately.

21 Q cuts all of the further exchanges, and the visit of Jamy and MacMorris from this scene, a total of 67 lines in F.

21.1 *and his lords* Llewellyn and Gower are given no exit here, so presumably they stay as part of the army for Henry's speech. The reviser Exeter can also be part of what F calls '*all his Traine*' here.

21.1 *Alarum* The stage direction alters F's '*Enter the King and all his Traine before the Gates*' by adding a singular '*alarum*'. This was presumably not meant to be the '*alarums and excursions*' of a battle scene, but signified a trumpet or drum–call summoning the Governor to the walls of Harfleur. Q3 re-positioned it at the beginning of the line, presumably to mark it as an order given in battle.

23 parley we'll Q's dissyllabic word is a more normal pronunciation than F's 'Parle'. The scansion is kept by eliding the verb.

25–7 Q's lineation slips here, as it often does before a long cut. See Appendix 1.

30 be F's 'lie' is more emphatic.

31 are F's 'shall be' is markedly more emphatic. The change loses Q the metre, but that is a characteristic loss just before a cut is made. The next thirty-one lines of Henry's threats against Harfleur if it does not surrender are taken out of the Q version.

35 succour Q simplifies the F plural, which may refer to the different sorts of help besides raising the siege that Holinshed reports the town asked for from the Dauphin.

36 not yet F's reversed order, elliptical for 'as yet', suggests a less ordinary excuse than Q's version.

40 defensive now Q's 'now' duplicates 'no longer', and the adjective loses the force of F's 'defensible'. The Q scene ends here, cutting Henry's orders about Exeter holding the town, and his statement about how weak his soldiers are. Q lacks any '*exit*' stage direction, although a version of F's descriptive '*Flourish, and enter the Towne*' might be expected.

Scene 7
Act 3 scene 5 in the NCS edition.

1 Q gives the French of this scene in a rough phonetic transcription that does not show a very intimate knowledge of French by the revisers. For this scene the Q text has been altered into, so far as it is possible to identify it, a rather more correct version of the broken French that the boys playing these two parts might have spoken. Mostly it is a reduced but not unfaithful paraphrase of the F scene.

2 *s'* Q's 'sae' is not easy to make into any correct French word here.

2 *anglais* Here Q inverts the language problem, and puts 'francoy'.

4 *la bras* Q has 'da', which suggests that it was made feminine, like 'la main'.

8 *s'appelez-vous* Q's 'Coman sa pella vow' adds a misleading 's' to its phonetic transcription, from F's 'Comient appelle vous'. The mistake is repeated at line 20.

10 *le* Q has 'de', the English version, which Alice copies in the next line.

11 *remembre* Q has 'Ie remembre', Franglais for 'je me rappelle'.

11 *le coude* Q has 'tude', possibly a compositor's wrong-fount error, since the two previous citations use 'c'.

13 *raconte* Adopted from its use at line 16. Q's word here, 'rehersera', is only slightly less erratic than 'remembre' in line 11. Q's invention is a memory of F's 'Ie men fay le repetitiõ'.

13 *apprendré* It seemed worth retaining the wrong past participle here, since it seems to show some knowledge of the main verb, apprendre. At the equivalent point F has 'apprins', which may either come from a reversed letter or a minim misreading by the compositor. Q's 'Iac apoandre' for 'J'ai appris' may reflect the compositor's difficulties here as much as the reviser's.

18 *comme si* Q has 'Asie', a mangled version of English 'as if'.

20 *Comment s'appelez-vous* Q has 'Coman se pella vou', as in line 8. F has 'coment appelle vous'.

23 fot In Q's spelling Katherine's echo of Alice's 'foot' seems to indicate a less than perfect pronunciation of the new word.

25 de . . . le Alice's use in Q of one English and one French pronunciation are retained here. F has 'le' in each case.

26 *est-il avisé* Q's text has 'et ill ausie'. The Franglais verb sums up Katherine's fifty words of horrified reaction in F.

Scene 8

Act 3 scene 6 in the NCS edition.

0.1 *the* DAUPHIN Q reduces the Dauphin's role in this scene, transferring to the Constable or cutting his F speeches. The only reason for his presence in Q is the king's order at the end of the scene to keep him from Agincourt, where he has one line of protest. While all the speeches are heavily trimmed, Bourbon retains his one speech from F.

2 sprays The Constable's 'spranes' in Q, possibly a compositor misreading of the minim in 'spraies', has been corrected here in deference to F's 'Sprayes'. The metaphor depends on line 4's 'grafters', which is in both texts. In F the Dauphin, who speaks these lines, picks it up from the Constable's 'Vineyards', which is cut from Q.

4 outgrow Q cuts two lines, which forces an alteration to the verb from F's 'And ouer-looke', referring to the sprays spurting upwards.

5–8 Q reduces Bourbon's five lines in F to four. F gives it to '*Brit.*', or Brittany, instead of Bourbon. See Introduction, p. 21.

5 *mortdieu*! Q's 'mor du' repeats the exclamation from line 2, which is close to F's '*Mort du ma vie*'. It is a standard if less intense exclamation than F.

8 short nook A rough but loyal paraphrase of F's peculiar 'nook-shotten'.

9–18 The Constable's lines are paraphrased throughout in Q. His condemnation of the climate and the preference for beer over wine are retained in roughly similar shape.

9 Why, Q cuts the Constable's initial phase in French, and replaces it with a much more commonplace exclamation.

11 disdain Q modifies the meaning of F's 'despight', putting scorn in place of revenge.

16 frozen icicles Q replaces F's 'roping Isyckles' with an anticipation of 'frosty' in the next line. F's word was repeated in 4.2, which Q omits, and is taken from Golding's translation of Ovid's *Metamorphoses* 1.136, a text studied at the upper levels in Tudor schools, where the reference is to 'icicles' which 'hung roping down'. The Q revisers did not recognise the model in Golding.

18 After the Constable's speech, Q cuts a five-line speech by the Dauphin and one of four by Bourbon.

19–20 The French king's twenty-line speech reciting the great names of the French nobles is cut entirely in Q, along with the Constable's four-line response. Instead two lines are invented in Q to summon the French herald, and his order to the Dauphin to stay with him is the last word in the scene.

19 Montjoy Q omits the identification supplied in F, '*Montioy* the Herald'.

20 ransom F makes no mention of ransom in this scene. Instead, the king speaks of Montjoy sending 'sharpe defiance'.

Scene 9
Act 3 scene 7 in the NCS edition.

0.1 *Enter* GOWER Q's omission of Llewellyn's name from this entry stage direction looks uncomfortably like similar possible omissions of his comings and goings in scene 6. His presence is marked in the dialogue, so is essential, and he is certainly not in the previous scene. This omission is more likely to have been a copyist's or reviser's error than the compositor's.

4 a man In transcription Q does lose one of the special locutions that were written into F for Llewellyn, his mouthing of polysyllables like 'magnanimous as *Agamemnon*'.

7 no . . . bridge Q adds Welsh phonetics, reproduced elsewhere in both texts, to F's 'any hurt in the World'. Llewellyn's idioms, such as Q's 'worell' here and his distinctive grammar 'is maintain', are not reproduced with entire consistency in either version. In this speech F's only phonetic spelling is 'Pridge', which first appears as 'Bridge'.

8 ensign Q uses the more modern form, while F has 'Aunchient Lieutenant', the pedantically exact title. He returns to the standard term at line 13.

8 I do . . . him See note to lines 12–13 below, and Introduction, p. 25.

10 reckoning F's 'estimation in the World' may have been composed to give

Llewellyn an extra occasion for his distinction pronunciation of 'worell'. If so, Q passed it up.

12–13 Such a question and its answer are anomalous, just after Llewellyn has announced in line 8 that 'I do not know how you call him'. This statement by Llewellyn is not in F, so in that text this question and answer are more fitting. On the other hand, Llewellyn does forget names twice elsewhere, at 16.7 (Macedon) and 28 (Falstaff), in both texts. This apparent contradiction in Q may simply have been Q's intensification of one of his mental traits.

13 Ancient F's spelling here and at lines 22, 36 and 38, is consistently 'Aunchient', which may echo the author's expectation of how Llewellyn would pronounce his name. If so, it is not reproduced in the Q spellings.

15 Do . . . him? Llewellyn aptly picks up Gower's denial, making the contradiction of line 8's insertion more conspicuous. Most likely in Q Gower the copyist is setting himself up for the statement about knowing Pistol after all at line 48.

19–21 As before, the last or cue line is exactly F's, but the rest is trimmed.

23 plind In a speech reproduced in Q with almost complete fidelity, F has 'blinde' on both its uses in this speech, while Q gives the Welsh pronunciation.

23 her F's version is 'his', which may be a compositor error or may have been intended as a joke, though Llewellyn's evidently knew his mythology precisely enough to give Dame Fortune the correct pronoun. Q gets it right.

25 variation, and mutabilities Q inverts the F sequence.

27 look you Q adds Llewellyn's catchphrase here.

29 pax This speech of Pistol's is as accurate as Llewellyn's preceding one. Its main divergence is the mishearing of 'pax' as 'packs'.

32 death Q normalises, probably because of the word in the previous line, F's 'Hempe'.

32 petty Q's adjective may have been a memory of the wordplay on petty/pretty at 1.113, where Q keeps 'petty'.

34 approach Q mishears F's 'reproach', and uses it, despite the nonsense it makes.

36 Captain In F Pistol is always identified correctly by his rank. This substitution in Q may be a copyist's mistake from its use in the previous line.

40 disciplines . . . kept Q intensifies by repetition F's 'discipline ought to be used'. The revised phrase may be an anticipation of Llewellyn's later assertion, at 11.24, when he protests that 'the auncient Prerogatiues of the warres be not kept'.

42 *figa* Q's 'figa', repeated at 11.20, F's '*figo*', is Pistol's Spanish for a fig, a common expression, though usually in English. Pistol translates his meaning at line 44. The correct form is 'fico'.

46 bowels . . . maw In F Pistol makes 44 his exit line. This extra parting shot is taken from his abuse of Nim at 2.33, where F has both 'bowels' and 'Maw'. Here the use of 'maw' makes a rhyme.

47 A strong elaboration of F's minimal response, 'Very good.'

48 the . . . of? Q refers back to the former discussion, whereas F's reviser merely says that Pistol is 'an arrant counterfeit Rascall'.

50 By Jesus Q is more exclamatory than F, using Llewellyn's most common oath. F's 'Ile assure you' does refer back to the earlier discussion.

50 prave . . . bridge F here gives 'praue' and 'Pridge'.

51 it's all one F uses another of Llewellyn's catchphrases, 'it is very well' in both places where Q gives him 'all's one'.

53–62 Q gives a close paraphrase of what was probably one of the reviser's speeches, dropping only a few short items.

56 scene Q's word stands in for F's less common 'Sconce', an earthwork fortification. For Q3's use of the same term, see Introduction, p. 8.

59 shout Q's word fits 'the camp' and its drunken noise more obviously than F's 'Sute', except for the link of F's reference to military clothing with beards cut in imitation of the camp's general. Square-cut 'Cadiz' beards, cut like the one worn by the Earl of Essex, were still fashionable throughout London in 1599.

63–5 Llewellyn's reply is only loosely equivalent to his lines in F. While giving the vague gist of F's lines, it adds a 'look you' catchphrase, and misses an opportunity to pronounce the 'Pridge' again.

65.1 *Enter . . . others* Q's stage direction seems to down-rate the flourish of banners and the tattered marching army which the F direction offers: '*Drum and Colours. Enter the King and his poore Souldiers.*'

67–8 Llewellyn's answer is far shorter, and therefore more deferential, than F's version, which has a 'looke you' and several plosives.

70 partition Q's spelling may be no more than a phonetic version of Llewellyn's pronunciation of F's 'perdition'.

72 man . . . church Q's version cuts F's 'one that is like to be executed', which leaves Bardolph's fate marginally less decided than in F. In view of the fact that Pistol has only just finished pleading for his life, F makes the better sense. Possibly the Q reviser was influenced by the end of the speech, which suggests that he has already been killed.

75 now Q's word is more positive than F's 'but'. The pious 'God be praised' before it is another Q insertion.

77–81 Q sets Henry's speech as verse, as it does everyone's in this scene. F sets it as prose, which has been adopted here.

77 we here give Q's expression is markedly stronger and more of an order than F's.

79 abused, or upbraided Another reversed doublet, for F's 'vpbrayded or abused'. Q's 'abraided' may be a mishearing. Q3 and F correct it to 'upbraided'.

80 gentlest F correctly has the comparative 'gentler'.

81.1 *Enter . . . HERALD* F's stage direction asks for a '*tucket*', the proper trumpet-call to announce a herald in his 'habit'.

83 we . . . we As in scene 1, the Q Henry uses the plural for his personal pronouns, where F uses the singular. His only use of 'I' in this scene is at line 97, after speaking of 'thy king' to Montjoy.

86–93 Q sets this speech as verse, like the rest, when it is clearly prose, as in F. It is a fairly accurate paraphrase, lacking only a few phrases in F, and one largish cut over the details of the ransom, the reference to France's 'losses' which England's Exchequer could not pay for, and the threat to Henry's soldiers, 'whose condemnation is pronounc't'. F's 'the Muster of his Kingdome' becomes in Q merely 'his army' at lines 90–1.

89 her . . . her F's 'his' makes 'England' into its king, not its people, which is Q's reading.

96 fair. Return Q retains the metre, against F's 'fairely. Turne'.

98 impeach Q misremembers these two lines, putting '*Callis*' before the risk of being stopped, and has to shorten F's 'impeachment' to keep the metre.

99 the sooth Q and F agree on the proverbial 'the sooth'. Conceivably it was originally 'to say thee sooth', but if so none of the printed texts read it that way.

103 army F's 'numbers' is more precise, and fits the following sentence better.

105 heart A possible misreading of F's 'health', the Q term loses the point of the statement at line 102 that they are enfeebled with sickness.

107 A short line in Q, exclamatory enough to stand on its own, but not set as one in F. As a result it generates mislineation down to line 109, and a final short line through an omitted word. See note to lines 114–17, and Appendix 1.

107 Frenchmen F's version makes better sense than the Q readings.

108 heir Q uses the spelling 'heire' which makes this pun clear on the page, while F uses the more basic 'ayre'.

110 Go tell Q omits F's 'therefore' between 'Go' and 'tell', an easy omission. In this passage's mislining the reviser seems to have relied on memory, while trying to maintain a reasonable scansion.

114–17 Misremembering produces a long line in Q at 114, and the next three lines are put together out of five in F, one of them also extra-syllabic. The misremembered lines in F begin with Henry giving Montjoy money, while it concludes them in Q's version. There is some point in Q's switch, since it generates a pun in what follows, at line 118, when Henry says 'The sum of all our answer . . .'

121 Q omits Henry's final 'So tell your master', to which Mountjoy responds here.

122 My Liege, Q adds this address. It has use in turning attention away from the exiting Mountjoy back to Henry and his lords.

122 now. Q2's question mark is less likely to reflect the intonation heard on stage than a misinterpretation of smudge in the Q1 text used as copy for Q2. Other such printing marks misled the Q2 compositor, such as the faint 'o' in 'con' at line 58 which was misread as 'can', and the blurred 's' at the end of 'fauours' at 3.4, which Q2 made into 'fauour:'.

124 Q makes one metrical line out of two in F.

125 This line, which does not make immediately good sense, is identical in F and Q. If there were more reliable instances it would seem to provide evidence that a copy of Q1, or its copy Q3, was used to set F. See Introduction, p. 9. Jackson's conjectural re-punctuation is attractive, but in the light of Q and F's agreement, and in the absence of more positive evidence for F borrowing from Q, the line must be presumed correct, and has been punctuated accordingly. It may have been designed to read, and been read as, 'give the order to march on the morrow'.

125.1 Q omits another '*Exeunt*' here.

Scene 10

Act 3 scene 8 in the NCS edition.

1 *Enter* ... GEBON In Q Bourbon replaces F's Dauphin, and 'Gebon' replaces Rambures. The contributions to the dialogue by Rambures are all cut. See Introduction, p. 21.

1 **world.** Q omits his plea 'would it were day', as it does the same complaint by Orleans three lines on, and Bourbon's (the Dauphin's) at the beginning of his first speech about his horse.

3–9 Bourbon's praise of his horse is abbreviated and greatly simplified in Q. His thirty-one lines with their responses in F become eight in Q. All the French phrases are cut.

7 **a the** Q several times uses 'a' to mean either 'has', 'hath' or 'of'. It seems worth retaining here, in preference to F's more standard 'of'.

10–23 Q cuts this set of witty exchanges from forty-nine lines in F to fourteen.

13–15 **shook ... me** Q's exchange is less bawdy than F's, where the Constable turns the Dauphin's counter that his mistress shook his back too with 'Mine was not bridled'. The Dauphin's attempt at a further response is cut in Q.

21 **Will ... morning?** This is the only wish for the night to end left in the Q version. It appears in F just before the Dauphin makes his exit, as here.

24.1 *Exit* F has an exit for the Dauphin marked here, and the dialogue makes it clear that Bourbon leaves. This is one of several exits that do not appear in the Q text.

25 GEBON His only contribution to the dialogue in this scene, it is notable because this line makes the scene's most meaningful change, from F's 'The Dolphin' to Bourbon. See Introduction, p. 21.

26–43 Q retains in rough form sixteen lines of badinage out of F's thirty-five, keeping the joke about eating all he kills and the exchange of proverbs. The proverb dialogue is switched with the joke about the Duke saying he is exceeding valiant, so that it interrupts F's flow from eating all he kills to his claiming valour.

44 **My lords** In F the messenger correctly addresses the Constable.

46 **Grandpere** Q's spelling seems to make a joke out of F's '*Grandpree*'.

47–8 F has another thirty-two lines of dialogue, mostly about the dog-like character of the English. Q retains the Constable's reply to the messenger, but replaces his second wish that day would come with a couplet from a later scene, F's 4.2, all of which is cut in Q bar this couplet. Its statement that that the sun is already high in the sky is rather too proleptic, since one of the wishes that day would come has been left in the Q text. See Introduction, p. 24.

47 **and an** The Q compositor fumbled here, possibly setting 'a' as the first letter of 'and', then thinking it was an ampersand, which he might have set with the full stop that follows the 'a'. Q2 sets an ampersand. Q3, setting from Q1, cuts out the mistake.

Scene 11

Act 4 scene 1 in the NCS edition.

1 For the cuts in Q that led to this entry, thirty-seven lines into Act 4 scene 1 in F, see Introduction, p. 23. Here, cutting the role of Erpingham means that Q only notes Henry is '*disguised*', and that they enter by opposing doors to meet onstage.

1 *Qui va la* F's '*Che vous la*', Q's 'Ke ve la' are roughly equivalent as phonetic versions
of French.

3 gentleman Q substitutes F's 'Officer' with the word Henry uses in the next line, and
Pistol of himself in line 8.

7 sir Here and at lines 15, 17 and 19 Henry addresses Pistol more respectfully than in
F.

9 Oh . . . king? Q presents Henry's reply as a mocking question, where in F it looks like
a more private witticism.

10 bago Q's word is a nonce-term, a vague memory of F's 'Bawcock'. Q omits one
phrase from this listing in F.

10 The Q compositor gives Pistol two speech headings on successive lines, at line 10
where his specch starts, and again where the next Q line starts at 'A lad of life'.

17 he . . . kinsman Q cuts Pistol's declaration that he will knock Llewellyn with a leek
in F and Henry's warning reply, an anticipation of what happens later.

20 *Figa* The same word and spelling in Q as at 9.42.

22 Pistol . . . name Q adds this comic repetition. In F Henry's line is spoken semi-
privately, as Pistol marches off. He stays onstage, to overhear first Gower and
Llewellyn and then the three soldiers.

24–8 Q marks Llewellyn's voice with 'worell' (F's 'World'), and possibly 'auncient' for
F's more eccentric spelling 'aunchient', but it misses F's 'pibble bable'. It also cuts
F's references to Pompey the Great and to the laws of war in F's 'aunchient Preroga-
tives and Lawes of the Warres'.

27 fears A human substitution for F's 'Formes'.

30 God's solud An addition by Q, 'sollud', varying Llewellyn's usual form of exclamation. This is probably a phonetic transcription by the Gower reporter of whatever oath the player of Llewellyn invented here.

36 this F specifies 'this Welchman', which makes a near-rhyme.

37 I SOLDIER Q removes the individual names that F, uniquely, gives to the three
soldiers. In F the first soldier (Alexander Court) begins by addressing 'Brother *Iohn
Bates*' by name, an obvious omission for Q.

43 KING. Now . . . cheer? Q gives no stage direction for Henry to come forward at
this moment. His brash greeting and his choice of the moment when the
third soldier (Bates in F) is wishing himself with the king in the Thames is drastically different from F's moment, when Williams gives him a formal sentry's challenge as a stranger, 'Who goes there?' Q's change also entails cutting the name of
Erpingham.

45 frolic Q alters the F version drastically, inserting this upbeat word and cutting
altogether's Henry's 128-word defence of the king as only a man.

47 The . . . smells In place of thirty lines of dialogue with Bates and Williams, Q takes
one sentence from Henry's long defence, and adds to it a lead-in for Williams's
speech about the concern if the king's cause is not good. It is a rather clumsy ellipsis,
since in F Henry bases his case on his assumption that the king's cause is good, the
point that Williams takes up at line 49.

49–53 Q trims F's 130 words down to 70. Q cuts the last sentence in F with Williams's point that soldiers have a duty to obey their king whatever the justice of his cause, and instead returns to the point he started with.

54–68 Again, Q trims F's 370 words down to 192. It keeps the gist very well, principally cutting adjectival phrases like '(peradventure)' and 'the Kings Quarrell'. It reverses the order of son before servant, shortening the servant's misfortunes and cutting F's 'Robbers'. Q also cuts the claim that no king has 'all vnspotted Souldiers' before specifying the types of spot, and as usual it cuts the final sentence in F, in this case about the value of God's lesson for those who survive the battle.

55 miscarry Q takes this word from F's account of the son.

57 lewd action Q's paraphrase for F's 'do sinfully miscarry'.

61 gift Q's misreading, or less possibly mishearing, for F's 'guilt'.

62 forgery Q's mistake for F's 'Periuie', possibly stimulated by the reference to writing in the 'broken seal'.

64 man's service Q substitutes the common term, possibly by infection from the mention of the 'servant' earlier in the speech, for F's 'Subiects Dutie'.

66 mote Q's 'moath' and F's 'Moth' may equally represent the spoken form of the word, which generates a pun also played on with the name of Moth in *Love's Labours Lost*.

69 3 SOLDIER On page D4v of Q the compositor mistakenly used '*Lord*' instead of his regular '*Sol.*' for the two speech headings at 69 and 72. See Introduction, p. 14.

69–70 Q compresses two F speeches, by Williams and Bates, into one here.

72 fight Q cuts the adjective from F's 'fight chearefully'.

75 Mass, Q gives Williams an exclamation not in F.

75–6 elder . . . cannon Q converts Williams's assertion in F that Henry's claim carries no more weight than a pop-gun into a simile of Henry with a pop-gun trying to injure Henry with a cannon, and converts the 'priuate displeasure' of a subject against a king into the pop-gun's derided 'great displeasure'.

76 monarch Q omits a Petrarchan comparison in F about turning the sun to ice by fanning it with a peacock's feather.

77 You're an ass Q's 'your a nasse' is a literal mishearing. F has the more moderate 'come, 'tis a foolish saying.'

78 bitter F's word 'round' is softer, just as Williams's dismissal in F is less scornful.

80 if . . . wilt A softer response in Q than F's 'if you liue'.

81 Q transfers the soldier's enquiry in F to Henry. This reverses the sequence of exchanges in the challenge that follows.

82 glove Q omits Henry's reference to the glove as a gage. In F Henry asks for a gage, and Williams offers a glove.

84 Q omits Williams's declaration in F that he will wear the glove in his hat, and Henry's claim that he will challenge it 'though I take thee in the Kings companie'.

87 no . . . broils Q loses Bates's jibe in F about having enough French quarrels already 'if you could tell how to reckon'.

88–9 Q cuts Henry's first sentence in Q but keeps the second. It then omits Henry's entire 'Ceremony' soliloquy and Erpingham's interruption at the end. For this cut and the reason for the intrusive stage direction at 89.1 in Q, see Introduction, p. 23.

The Q3 editor or compositor tried to make sense of it by inserting '*to*', so that the lords enter to the onstage Henry. Q1, followed by Q3, places the soldiers' exit later than F, which leaves the king making his joke about clipping French crowns to their departing backs.

90–103 Q cuts the last two lines of this speech, and compresses others, trimming F's eighteen lines to fourteen. Q's version has some mislineation (see Appendix 1), and some paraphrasing, such as 'May not appal their courage' for F's 'Pluck their hearts from them' at line 93.

93–4 Oh . . . God Q reverses the precise form of F's repetition, making it simpler, with less of the heavy sigh required by F's first 'o' in the middle of the repetition.

94 think on Q omits F's intensive 'thinke not vpon'.

97 have F's 'haue' makes better grammatical sense than Q's 'hath', a copyist's error.

99 A . . . men Q reduces F's 'Fiue hundred poore', also shrinking F's 'twice a day' to 'every day' at line 100.

102 chantries As so often towards the end of a long speech, Q economises on F. One and a half lines about the 'solemne Priests' at the chantries along with Henry's own pentience are cut. The substitution of 'chanceries' for F's chantries may be a mishearing.

103 all . . . little Q's trimming loses F's underlying image that Henry, on his knees as he is in his prayer, is doing the penitent's act of following Richard's funeral procession on his knees asking for pardon.

104 Lord Q normalises F's 'liege'.

107 Stay . . . stay Q alters the tone of Henry's response to his brother. In F, he recognises who is speaking in a questioning voice, and says slowly and wearily 'I: I know thy errand'. Q's version, picking up his first word as an anticipation from one in his last line, is far more urgent. Q's words go with his leaping urgently to his feet and into movement offstage.

108 stay Q's 'stayes' may have been written as a plural to differentiate it from the imperatives with which the speech starts.

Scene 12

Act 4 scene 3 in the NCS edition.

0.1 The first of three anomalous re-entries in Q, Gloster's arrival here immediately follows his exit with Henry in the previous scene. Conceivably, since Henry only acknowledges his 'voyce', he did no more then than appear briefly at the door. In F a scene with the French lords intervenes. See Introduction, p. 11.

1 WARWICK In F this speech is Westmorland's, after eighteen lines of dialogue among the lords about the odds. Cutting him from Q gives it to Warwick, who is not recorded in the entry stage direction. Like the survival of the F stage direction at 11.89, it indicates some rather cursory revision by the Q revisers at this point.

2 Exeter retains in Q the odds named in F, but Warwick's figure in line 3 shrinks from Westmorland's F total of sixty thousand ('threescore') to forty. Q switches the sequence of these lines, in which the figures are as close as Q gets to the F text.

4–6 In Q, given that he has to alter all but one of the names, Salisbury preserves nothing of his F lines except for a paraphrase of his farewell.

7–9 Clarence's three lines in Q, taken from Exeter in F, retain one line, and paraphrase the third. The farewells should precede exits – in F Salisbury's last word is 'adieu' – but the king's entry and his interruption of Warwick's speech suggests that Salisbury is held back, and nobody leaves. There is no exit stage direction in either text.

10 but . . . thousand Warwick, taking Westmorland's lines from F, misreads F's figures. His words re-interpret F's fraction, one in ten thousand, as a simple number.

12–15 Warwick's speech in Q ends in a full line, where in F it ends as a half-line which Henry completes. The change loses Henry's metre, and leads to two short lines. This edition retains Q's lineation here, because the scansion and wording of its text is too far from F to make any re-lineation possible.

13 God's will An exclamation displaced by Q's deletion from F along with its sequel 'I pray thee', of Henry's case that those present are enough loss to England if they die. In Q he offers only the larger share-out of honour amongst the few.

15 This line is not in F.

16 No, faith Q invents an oath for F's 'Gods will' here.

16 After this line Q omits ten lines from F, picking the grammar up again neatly with 'Rather' in the next line.

17 presently An insertion by Q after the ten-line cut. It keeps the metre, replacing this line's cut of Westmorland's name.

23 day of Q repeats 'day' from earlier in the line in place of F's 'Feast'.

24 sees old age Q reverses the phrases in Henry's trope, substituting here F's 'comes safe home' from line 27. Q's use of the phrase from F's line 24 lacks the auxiliary 'shall' which F has there, so simplifies the verb here to 'see'.

26 Crispin Although the metre here and at line 23 calls for F's version, Q uses the alternative spelling 'Crispin'. See Introduction, p. 9.

27 outlives Q repeats the same phrase from line 24, while F varies it with 'shall see'.

27 comes safe home In this repetition F has 'liue old age', the verb taking up the 'shall' earlier in the same line.

29 Crispin's Day F has the same metre, with '*Crispian*'.

30 Q's last nineteen lines of this speech paraphrase F's twenty. Line 30 is taken from eight lines below, the list of names following comes from six and seven below, then follow two more misplaced lines (34 and 35), and one very roughly paraphrased (36). Line 37 and the four following are taken from the last eight lines in F. Lines 42 and 43, the latter invented, are from the two immediately after line 29 in Q. The last five lines garble the last four in F.

32 Bedford . . . Gloster Q retains the first name from F, despite cutting Bedford from the text, and substitutes Clarence for Warwick, Gloster for Talbot, and Warwick and York for Salisbury and Gloster in the next line. This is a fairly rough replacement of the parts cut from F. Warwick and York are added because they have speaking parts in Q. F's Talbot belonged in *1 Henry VI*, not at Agincourt, so was very properly cut, but Salisbury has a speaking part in Q in this scene.

34 their mouths Q alters the F text because of the alterations. The plural echoes 'their flowing bowls' of line 30. Q has to change F's singular 'his mouth', who is the old man remembering, but who in Q does not show his scars until line 42 below.

36 general doom Q's scansion problems have grown in the transcription, so that F's 'ending of the World' needed abbreviation.

38 bond Q's spelling reminds us that 'bond' and F's 'band' were cognate, as the wordplay on them in *The Merchant of Venice* and *King Lear* shows. As both of those plays show, a 'bond' was often sealed with blood.

39 by mine Q indicates a more literal-minded view of shedding blood on a battlefield than F's 'with me'.

40 base F's 'vile' intensifies the extent of the social gulf between a common soldier and a king, and the concession that Henry is promising, to turn every soldier into a gentleman, as the next line specifies.

42 Q transfers this from the beginning of the re-lineation, at line 30. The line following has been adopted by editors since Malone as part of the F text, on the grounds that it was accidentally omitted in printing.

43 Most editors have accepted Q's line, on the assumption that F omitted it through compositor error.

45 Q3 has an intriguing insertion here. The phrase 'They were not there' is remarkably close to F's 'they were not here'. See Introduction, p. 9.

49 GLOSTER F gives this to Salisbury, as a three-line speech. In F he was farewelled at line 7 (TLN 2252), although F marks no exit for him, so it is logical that he should now enter as the only lord not already on stage. Q appears not to have been concerned that anyone need enter to make this announcement.

50 Why Q adds this exclamation to the line, otherwise the same as F's.

51 WARWICK F gives this line to Westmorland.

52 cousin This form of address is correct for F's Westmorland, not Q's Warwick.

54 battle out Q's version of F's 'Royall battaile' is a more ordinary paraphrase.

55 KING Why Q gives this as the catchword at the end of the previous page (E2), but omits the speech heading from the start of the new page.

55 well said F's 'now thou hast vnwisht fiue thousand men' is more colourful, but it gives the sort of figure that Q avoids.

59 What . . . ransom? Q is very blunt. F's version, 'If for thy Ransom thou wilt now compound', is more conditional. F follows it with seven further lines, cut in Q, assuring Henry of his overthrow and advising his 'followers' to repent, as if they were heretics.

62–93 Q paraphrases this longest of Henry's F speeches fairly closely, and accurately. Only two blocks of three lines are cut in Q.

64 good Q consistently replaces F's 'poore' with this word throughout.

68 Find . . . France Q lengthens F's 'Native Graues', and cuts the next two lines in F and the first half of F's line 69, giving Q's line an extra-metrical syllable.

74 abundant Q normalises F's 'abounding'.

75 crazing Q and F agree on this unusual word, both spelling it 'crasing'. Their proximity with such a rare word suggests possible consultation of the manuscript by the Q revisers for this speech.

77 Q reproduces F's difficult line, often modified by editors, more precisely than usual, further possible evidence for direct consultation of the F manuscript.

78 Let . . . proudly Q's short line exactly reproduces F, but Q cuts the remainder of the line and the three following.

79 camp Q's word, used commonly elsewhere in both texts, is more workaday than F's 'Hoast'.

85 clothes F 'Coats'. A soldier's 'coat' showed the company he belonged to, usually his commander's colours. Losing their coats would then 'turn them out of service'. Q's 'cloathes' is a more neutral term.

87–8 Q rephrases F's assertion about 'my Ransome', turning it from the personal to the general. It is unclear whether Q's 'our' is meant to refer to the army generally, or to Henry in the royal plural.

91 nought i.e., nothing. F's 'none' means more specifically 'no ransom'.

91 bones Q's word is much more standard than F's 'ioynts'.

92 'em them This awkward locution is almost the same in both texts, Q 'am them', F 'vm them'.

94 Q cuts Montjoy's addition in F that Henry 'neuer shalt heare Herald any more', and Henry's reply that he will come back again for a ransom.

Scene 13

Act 4 scene 5 in the NCS edition. Q switches this scene and the next, possibly for casting reasons.

0.1 The four lords are those from scene 10. Their speeches are redistributed fairly randomly in Q.

1 *diabolo* Q's only attempt to reproduce the French of the French lords, this word is Spanish, a rough equivalent for F's '*Diable*'.

2 *Mort . . . vie* Q's Constable takes this phrase from F's Dauphin. In this scene Bourbon replaces the Dauphin only with an invented line (4), and then the speech that was originally Bourbon's in F.

5 CONSTABLE Q gives a speech by Orleans from the end of the scene to the French commander much earlier.

8 A . . . order Q paraphrases Bourbon's last speech in F, replying to Orleans ('The diuell take Order now'), before launching him into his main speech from F.

10 home Q puts more emphasis on the word than F's 'hence'.

11 leno A sophisticated non-English version of F's 'Pander'. Used by Nashe in *Have With You to Saffron Walden*, published in 1596, this word has been taken as evidence for authorial revision in Q.

13 contaminate F's 'contaminated' gives the basic word, and the metre demands the shorter form. Q's 'contamuracke', which is metrically correct, looks very like a misreading.

14–18 Q gives the last exhortation to the French commander, the Constable. The first

two lines are straight from the F text, the third an invention, and the fourth is
Bourbon's final line from F's version of the scene.

18 Let's . . . honour F's version of this is 'Let life be short', initiating a wordplay on
a long shame against a short life which Q overlooks.

Scene 14
Act 4 scene 4 in the NCS edition.

1 Yield . . . cur! In Q Pistol intensifies F's single order.

2 Q cuts an initial ten lines from the F version, with its first of three jokes about Pistol
misunderstanding the Frenchman.

3 'Moy' In most regions of France in 1599 a number of vowels were pronounced
differently from modern French. The modern 'oi' as in 'toi' and 'moi' was spoken
more like 'oy' as in 'toy'. Pistol, using the second of F's three language jokes, hears
'moiety', a half. Q cuts the third language joke in F after this comment.

5 The Boy's command of French is less than perfect in both versions. Here Q does
reproduce the F text. The reflexive verb was less standard in sixteenth-century
French.

7 Fer The Frenchman's name, in F and Q, simply means 'man of iron', which
underlines the comic and jingoistic game played with his terror. It may also have a
connection with Pistol's inexplicable but most likely obscene phrase dismissing his
new wife's request at 4.2.

14 fox Q takes up an earlier phrase in F, emphasising Pistol's flourishing of his ancient
broadsword, a bastard sword or 'fox'. Because it was set in Q1 as a turnunder on a
line below, the Q2 compositor saw it as a stage direction.

15–20 Q's French here is distinct from F's, not only for its inaccuracy. Q also misplaces
the speech heading for the Boy, transferring the first part of his reply to M. Fer to
the Frenchman. The Frenchman's next speech is in a very broad paraphrase. It has
none of F's references to him pleading on his knees, it calls Pistol a *'grand captaine'*
instead of a *'Chevalier'*, and it specifies a ransom of fifty *'écus'*.

19 *avez* Q's word 'auez' has no exact equivalent in F. Either the modern infinitive
'avoir' following 'pour', or the omission of 'pour', would be more correct than Q's
French here.

23 five . . . crowns The Boy in Q reports the Frenchman's offer in line 18 of a ransom,
but multiplies it tenfold.

25 cur In Q, not F.

25 Q cuts the Boy's last soliloquy to the audience.

Scene 15
Act 4 scene 6 in the NCS edition.

0.1 At the end of scene 13, immediately preceding this scene in F, the stage direction
specifies '*Alarum*', the only direct indication of battle in the F version. It is followed
by the direction opening this scene, '*Enter the King and his trayne, with Prisoners*'. Q's
version, which comes after scene 14 with Pistol and his prisoner, has no sound of
battle, and marks an entry for '*the King and his Nobles*, Pistoll', and no prisoners.
This, a consequence of Q's reversal of F's scenes 13 and 14, requires Pistol to leave

and immediately re-enter. See Introduction, p. 25. Only the king and Exeter among the lords speak in this scene. Neither Q nor F specifies who else is in the '*trayne*'. Gloster and Warwick are the most likely other entrants, here and at the similar entry direction in the next scene.

1 What ... retire Q invents a short sentence in place of F's less-committed praise. The change contradicts itself, claiming the French retreat and yet keep the field.

4 Twice Q reduces F's 'thrice'.

5 Q shortens the second of Henry's three lines in F.

11 hasted Q's word is an invention, replacing F's equally vivid portmanteau word, 'hagled ouer', for 'hacked' and 'mangled'. Q's version mixes 'hacked' and 'pasted'.

12 steeped By cutting the prefix that F has, Q loses the metre.

15 And cried Q here alters the tense with which the account started, at line 7 and 12. F maintains the present tense.

17 awhile F's 'for mine' is more purposive.

17 to rest Q's phrase has the same sound as F's 'a-brest' but a different meaning.

20 them Since Suffolk is dead, York is the only one that Exeter can cheer up, so Q's alteration of F's 'him' is wrong here.

21 He ... hand Q cuts F's one and a half lines to one half-line here.

24–7 so espoused ... Forced Q omits a phrase and has to re-line the text with one short and two long lines.

25 an argument F's 'Testament' is better fitted to the metaphor about sealing a contract with blood. Duthie (p. 122) considers that the transposition came from a memory of Henry's Harfleur speech (TLN 1104–5), where in F the word 'attest' adjoins 'argument'. That whole speech is omitted from Q.

28 had Q1, copied by Q2, omits this word. Since its loss damages both sense and metre, it must be a compositorial slip. Q3's correction, also in F, was a sensible change.

29 my mother Q and F agree on a more personal pronoun than was usual with this medical term.

31 For ... tears Q reduces two lines to one, cutting a phrase in F, 'mixtfull eyes', that has baffled editors.

31.1 *Alarum sounds* The only battle signal sounded offstage in the Q stage directions. F has two, at the beginning and end of this scene.

32 this? Bid Q omits the F line explaining why Henry gives his order: 'The French haue re-enforc'd their scatter'd men'. It also omits the connective 'Then', replacing it with the imperative 'Bid'.

33 *Couple gorge!* A much-debated addition in Q, and the only justification for including Pistol in the scene. See Introduction p. 27. Q sets it in roman, as it does in all the scenes where French is spoken.

Scene 16

Act 4 scene 7 in the NCS edition.

1 God's plood Q adds this exclamation to the F text. In F Llewellyn's first word closely echoes Henry's word for the prisoners, which Q's addition loses. Q also adds 'in the worell now' to F, as one of Llewellyn's catchphrases.

3–7 Gower's revision of what we have seen led Henry to give his order is almost exactly the same in Q as in F.

7 worthy F's 'gallant' is marginally more two-edged than Q's word.

8 born F gives him his Welsh pronunciation here, with 'porne'.

9 place Q normalises F's 'Townes name'.

12 reckoning ... variation F intensifies Llewellyn's idiosyncrasies by making both of these words plural.

15–24 Q reproduces almost the same text as F, with only one cut, of a sentence about comparisons between the two cities, the transfer of 'it' for '*Alexanders* life' to its second use, the specification 'our king' instead of 'Harry of Monmouth', and the point that Alexander was intoxicated. The one 'look you' is located differently in Q than in F.

16 worell Q's spelling is the standard one for Q's transcriptions. F makes it 'Orld'.

19 brain F has the more phonetic 'pranes'.

21 an Q has 'and'; F uses 'If'.

25 Ay, but Gower's exclamation is an addition by Q, as is the conjunctive 'for'.

27 Look you An addition in Q. F instead has '(marke you now)' after Llewellyn's start to his sentence, which Q does not copy.

28 in ... comparisons F has 'but in the figures, and comparisons of it'.

29 is kill Q has the Welsh idiom more strongly. F merely has 'kild'.

29 Clitus Q omits Llewellyn's qualifier, F's 'being in his Ales and his Cuppes', which justifies the second half, retained in Q, that Henry by contrast was in his right mind.

33 Aye ... indeed Q's repetition of the name is not in F.

34 Q omits Gower's warning that the king is coming.

34.1 F's stage direction here is confusing. It signals an offstage '*alarum*', not in Q, to show that the battle is still going on, and in this and its other indications almost repeats the stage direction at the beginning of scene 15, the entry of the English nobles '*with prisoners*'. The only difference is that this stage direction specifies '*Burbon*' to accompany the king. Q's entry direction is also imperfect. It mentions no prisoners, and gives no entry for Williams (2 SOLDIER), who is required on stage later in the scene.

36 hour Q loosens the time-constraint from F's 'instant', allowing Henry's anger time to emerge from the news about the French raid on the English baggage train.

39 leave F's 'voyde' is the more vivid word. Q normalises.

41 skir Q's 'skyr' is very close to F's 'sker', an exceptional word.

42 enforced Q mislines slightly here, although it keeps the metre. F spells the word 'Enforced', the metre demanding a stress on the final syllable. Q's mislining calls for only a two-syllable word here, reflected in the Q spelling 'enforct'.

44 Q trims two lines of F to one, cutting the final half-line which sends the English herald off.

44.1 When Montjoy enters, in F Exeter announces his arrival, and Gloster comments on his humbler aspect. Both lines are cut in Q.

46 ransom? Q omits F's repetition by Henry in the next line, 'Com'st thou againe for ransome?'

47 favour Q makes Montjoy's reply less flat. In F he first answers Henry by saying 'No great King', and asks for 'License', not a favour.

49–50 In F Montjoy asks first to 'booke' and only then to bury the French dead. Line 49 in F comes after its version of line 50, as an explanation of the wish to 'booke' the French nobles.

49 We may Q gets confused as a result of its switch of lines 49 and 50. Consequently it is not clear whether line 49 starts as a direct request, with the noun and verb reversed, or whether it is meant to be an expansion of the preceding request. In F it is the latter, and the line begins 'That we may', which is what the Q reporter remembered.

50 Q replaces the next nine lines of Montjoy's speech in F with its own one-line summary in line 47.

53 keep Q compresses Henry's specification of the French horsemen who 'peere, And gallop' over the battlefield.

54–5 These two half-lines in Q make a metrically correct single line, the first compressed from Henry's F couplet. The next two half-lines, however, the first also compressed from a full line by Henry, would contain twelve syllables if taken together. It is doubtful whether the Q revisers intended the four half-lines to match together as single lines, so they have been kept separate in this edition.

59 Crispin, Crispin Q's doubling of what elsewhere is the single name has provoked major speculation about its meaning and its cause. F's '*Crispin Crispianus*', which is identical to the revision in Q3, reflects uncertainty about the name of the shoemaker's two patron saints. See Introduction p. 9.

60 grandfather Q cuts the citation in F of King Edward's son the Black Prince.

62 'Tis true Q adjusts to suit the cut of the prince's name. F acknowledges the mention of two heroes with 'They did'.

64 leeks . . . grow Q omits the reference to wearing leeks in Monmouth caps.

72 so long . . . man Q omits Llewellyn's statement that he need not be ashamed of Henry, the prelude to this condition.

73 me so F has an entry direction for Williams at this point. Q supplies none.

74 scattered French In F Henry asks for the 'numbers dead / On both our parts.' Q then sends the English and French heralds off together to make the tally of both sides, as Henry instructs and as the plural in the stage direction shows.

75–6 soldier . . . fellow In F the king asks for the 'fellow', and Exeter orders the 'soldier' to come. In Q Llewellyn's condescending 'fellow' anticipates his attitude to Williams later.

77 Fellow Q reverts to 'fellow' where in F Henry makes him 'Souldier'.

78–80 Q compresses two replies by the Soldier in F into one.

82–4 Q cuts and paraphrases Llewellyn in F, here and in lines 86–7, taking the 'blacke shoo' from the later speech.

95–7 Like everyone's speech in Q, Henry's prose is set as verse here. This edition follows the F setting.

96 was Q3 made the Q1 verb agree with its noun. The fact that F had the right plural in the first place does not justify its use here.

102 An . . . Majesty Q makes this another of Llewellyn's characteristic phrasings added to the F wording. He repeats it at line 105.

105.1 Q omits this exit, which is marked in F.

106 In F Henry tells Warwick and Gloster by name to follow Llewellyn.

107 Q omits a line saying that Llewellyn might get his ear boxed.

108–12 Q trims F's ten lines down to five, in a rough paraphrase which takes three lines almost intact from F.

112.1 No exit is given here in Q, but there is one in F, and Q gives a re-entrance for Henry and his nobles eight lines later. Q must have intended a scene break here.

Scene 17

Act 4 scene 8 in the NCS edition.

0.1 In F Williams enters with Gower first, Williams predicting to Gower that he has been sent for so that he can be knighted. Llewellyn meets them from the other door. Q merges Williams's story into Llewellyn's. He most likely hurries in as in F from the other door to meet Gower and his man.

6 God . . . his Q's addition makes Llewellyn's exclamation more idiomatic than F's plain 'Sblud'. It is possible that Q's 'Gode' is a compositor misreading or a scribal mistranscription of an intended 'Gods'.

7 Q omits eight lines from F, including Gower's intervention, Williams's defence against Llewellyn's charge of treason and Llewellyn naming Alençon.

7.1 In F, Warwick and Gloster enter first, followed by Henry and Exeter five lines later. Q's grouped entry nullifies Henry's order to Warwick at 16.106 to hurry ahead in case of trouble. Warwick's initial demand to know what is happening is cut in Q along with Llewellyn's four-line reply so that all four nobles can enter together.

9–13 Q conflates two speeches in F by Llewellyn, and makes Williams's defence against the first speech follow.

16 that gentleman In F the soldier calls him 'this man'.

18–19 Q keeps only the first sentence from Llewellyn's second speech in F here, transferring the rest to his first speech.

20–1 Q shortens both lines. They are both short of a full metrical line-length in F, and may have been intended as prose, before Henry's verse resumes at line 22.

24 How . . . amends? Q cuts a line by Llewellyn that precedes this question in F, attaching it to Henry's previous grave speech, and puts it after. F's version of the line is metrically perfect verse, even though it is separated in F from his previous couplet.

25 marshal's The Q scribes failed to understand Llewellyn's reference to martial law, which would be used to determine the punishment for striking an officer.

26–32 Q merges two speeches by the soldier, omitting Henry's interceding comment that 'It was our selfe thou didst abuse', which the Q statement 'your self came not like your self', not in F, takes up.

33–7 Neither Q nor F makes very good verse of these lines, even though F sets it as verse. Conceivably it could have been written to be prose, reflecting the sudden drop in the regal pose. This edition retains it as verse.

38 By Jesus In F Llewellyn has a remarkable new oath, 'By this Day and this Light', which Q normalises.

39–40 brawls and brabbles F's version spells this 'prawles and prabbles'.

41 sir, not I The F version of this line is terse, even sulky. It uses no form of address. The Q version allows the rejection to end with a touch of upbeat defiance.

42 squeamish The word in F is 'pashfull'.

44 The Q text turns directly to the naming of the French prisoners, as if Exeter had been patiently holding the list while Henry's game with the soldier went on. It omits to mark any entry for the herald who in F delivers the paper. In F Henry takes the list of the French dead and then asks Exeter to name the prisoners of the nobility. He then reads out the list of dead, starting at what Q, by omitting the speech heading, makes into Exeter's fifth line. Whether Q omits the speech heading for the king at line 49 or whether it was meant to be at line 59, the two possibilities indicated in the text, Exeter's line at the end makes it clear that a speech heading for Henry is omitted somewhere in Q. F gives the speech starting at line 49 to Henry, and that has been adopted here. See note to line 59.

51 F has nine lines giving the numbers of the French dead; Q omits them, giving only the list of noble names which follows in F.

52 de la Brute In F this is '*Delabreth*'.

54 John, Duke Alençon F exchanges the name for this role with Rambures, who appears in the French scenes in F, and is cut in the Q version. Q names him next, without any special title. Alençon figures in Henry's story to Llewellyn about the glove.

56 Nobelle Charillas Q's addition, not in F. Conceivably after copying from F the name 'Dauphin' the Q revisers thought that the man's name needed clearer identification. It appears nowhere in Holinshed. 'Nobelle' may be the reviser's phonetics for French 'noble'. The nearest name to 'Charillas' in the Chronicles is Philip of Charolais, son to the Duke of Burgundy, who was not at Agincourt but according to the *Gesta Henrici Quinti* received the spoils from the raid on the baggage camp at Agincourt. He succeeded his father in 1619, and was the Duke of Burgundy present at the Treaty of Troyes, featured in scene 19. How the revisers found such a name is an open question.

58 Gerard and Verton These names in Q replace '*Beaumont* and *Marle*' in F. They do not appear in Holinshed either. Barbara Damon Simison, 'A Source for the First Quarto of *Henry V*', *MLN* 46 (1931), 514–15, pointed out that there is a 'Gerard' listed among the French dead in *The Brut*'s account of Agincourt. There is no Verton amongst its list of 108 names (which includes 'The Lord Dauphyon'), nor any 'Charillas'.

59 Both Q2 and Q3 independently solved the problem of speech attribution by reintroducing Henry here, so that Exeter could reply at line 70.

62 Ketly Identical in F and Q, the origin of this name has exercised editors. It is not in Holinshed, the source of the other names.

63 Q omits F's 'None else of name' at the beginning of this line.

64 Q makes this a half-line, as in F. Cutting F's phrase at line 63 left it a full line, which might have allowed it to become the first half of a pair of half-lines. F, however, sets the two half-lines on separate lines, making line 64 in both texts a short line to itself.

65 Q compresses a line and a half into one line here, using 'Thee' to avoid the repetition of 'thy Arme' in F. The cut leaves the Q text with a half-line at 66.

65–9 Q's cut of a half-line at 65 leads to re-lineation of F's lines for the rest of the speech.

71 let us go Q adjusts F's 'goe me', which is probably a compositor's slip for 'go we'.

72 to any man Q alters F's 'through our Hoast'.

76 Llewellyn Q reminds us of his name. In F Henry here and elsewhere addresses him as 'Captaine'.

Scene 18

Act 5 scene 1 in the NCS edition.

1 The beginning of Act 5 in F, this scene ignores Henry's triumphant return to England celebrated by the Chorus, and goes straight to the settling of scores after Agincourt which opens the Act that follows the Chorus.

1 Both F and Q give the two captains an entry in mid-speech, which means by the same door. That frees the other for Pistol to enter and meet them.

2–6 F's version is longer than Q's here. Q omits Llewellyn's statement that he is wearing a leek in his cap, and transfers some of F's long list of the imprecations he applies to Pistol's name to his second speech, when he is addressing Pistol directly.

12–13 Q shortens Llewellyn's long sentence, but adds the address 'Antient *Pistoll*', here and at line 15.

17 Q shortens the sixty-three words of Q to seventeen here.

21 F adds a sentence addressed to Pistol about the leek being good for his 'greene wound' and 'ploodie Coxecombe'.

23.1 The editor or compositor of Q3, whose enthusiasm for adding touches to the Llewellyn scenes grew as the play goes on, added the graphic but hardly necessary stage direction here.

24 Good, good Q simplifies Pistol's response. F gives Pistol a single 'Good' in reply to Llewellyn's speech at line 21 that is omitted by Q. In F's version Pistol switches his ground, starting 'I will most horribly reuenge', and without any punctuation break going on to say 'I eate and eate I sweare'. Two further exchanges are omitted by Q.

25 shilling The sum Llewellyn offers in F is a groat, worth only a third of the shilling he offered to Williams.

26 bloody coxcomb Picked up by Q from the speech cut at line 21, for F's 'pate'.

29 reckoning Q's Pistol turns it into a financial bargain from F's 'reuenge'.

31 buy Q omits the explanatory phrase in F here, 'buy nothing of me but cudgels', confusing the issue and the purchase image by spelling it 'by'.

33.1 Q gives no exit for Gower, although Pistol's last speech is spoken alone. It cut Gower's last ten-line diatribe to Pistol, and, if the copyist here was making use of the F manuscript, must have taken out his '*Exit*' direction at the end of it with the rest.

34–43 The first line of Pistol's final soliloquy is his parting shot at Llewellyn's departure. The rest comes after Gower's diatribe in F and his departure. F sets it as prose, which it certainly is, up to the last couplet, which is in rhyme. In fact all of lines 35–43 in Q's version scan in perfect decasyllables, and have been set out here as verse, following Q's lineation, except that Q sets line 41 as two short lines.

35 hussy Probably a written form of the transitional pronunciation, which moved from F's 'huswife' through Q's 'huswye' to the nineteenth-century 'hussy'.

36 warlike lines F has 'wearie limbes', where it is a statement, not a question, and it follows the statement about Doll's sickness.

38 Doll Q copies F in ignoring Pistol's wife Nell Quickly and referring only to Doll Tearsheet.

38 One malady F's prose puts her 'i'th Spittle of a malady of France', which makes better sense than Q's 'sicke. One mallydie of *France*.' But Q's line is metrical, and has been retained here.

39–40 An invention in Q, the word 'home' in line 39 may refer more directly to his resource with Mistress Quickly than does F's statement that Doll's death quite cuts off 'my rendeuous'. Q merely says that she is 'sicke'. Q also omits F's 'Old do I waxe', transferring F's reference to his honour being cudgelled from here to line 36, although it turns F's 'Cut-purse of quicke hand' to 'the sleight of hand' (Q 'slyte of hand') in line 40.

42 these scars Q omits F's adjective 'cudgeld', which is extra-metrical.

Scene 19
Act 5 scene 2 in the NCS edition.

0.1–3 Q's direction that the opposing parties enter by opposing doors may suggest that for the harmonious conclusion they should exit in pairs through the central opening.

0.1 KATHERINE Q names her 'Queene Katherine'. Q cuts Queen Isabel, who is named in F's entry direction, and has a speaking part. The '*Queene*' in Q's stage direction may be a relic from the original manuscript.

0.3 BOURBON Q confuses the Duke of Bourbon, who stands in for the Dauphin at Agincourt, with the Duke of Burgundy, the peacemaker at Troyes.

1 SH Q's speech headings for Henry in this scene are '*Harry*' or '*Har*' (and once '*Hate*'), because of the presence of the French king, who is consistently '*France*' or '*Fran*'.

7 we Q gives the French king the royal 'we', when he should be welcoming the English nobles as 'you'. F has it correctly.

7 Q, cutting the French queen altogether, omits her welcome.

8–11 Q cuts Burgundy's speech about peace in France from forty-five lines in F to four. Q invents the first line of the four, and paraphrases the last three.

10 rub or bar Burgundy in F uses 'rub' in his eleventh line. He uses 'bar' in his fifth to mean the present scene, 'this Barre, and Royall enterview', where it means a lawcourt or legal bar, not a doublet for 'rub', or block, as it becomes in Q.

13–14 Q paraphrases, reducing F's five lines and giving only the gist. Q then cuts Burgundy's intercession over the Articles and Henry's impatient reply, allowing the French king to respond directly.

15 cursenary The reporter may have guessed at Q's word from its sound. F's 'curselarie' suggests that the F compositor had a similar difficulty. Modern editors turn it into 'cursitory', a variant form of 'cursory'.

18 our peremptory Q compresses into one manageable adjective F's not very grammatical doublet, 'our accept and peremptorie'.

19–20 Q compresses F's eight lines, naming five English lords, and specifying how much freedom they have to 'Augment or alter' the Articles.

21 Q omits Henry's reason, that Katherine is 'our capital Demand'. Q has already cut the offer of her hand mentioned by the third Chorus, which adds that 'The offer likes not'.

22.1–2 Q's stage direction is more specific and accurate than F's, which follows '*Exeunt omnes*' with a '*Manet*' only for Henry and Katherine, ignoring Alice.

23–30 In F Henry starts with four lines of verse, to which Katherine replies in prose, before they both continue in prose. Most of the opening exchanges in F are omitted in Q, which starts nearly forty lines on.

25 compare with any Q softens Henry's bawdy joke about leaping into a wife. It picks out only two details from his later speeches in F, about having him at the worst and wearing him better, and begetting a boy who can go on a crusade.

31 This reply from Katherine comes at the end of Henry's first long speech in F, as it does here in Q. Henry's answer in Q is a close paraphrase of F.

36 what Q copies F closely here, although F spells it 'wat', phonetically.

37–9 Q compresses Henry's attempt at French in F considerably. Instead of F's extensive attempts at Franglais, Q launches a translation exercise, not in F, where Katherine translates each phrase of Henry's French into her English.

47–8 Q takes this from the end of the speech by Henry paraphrased in lines 37–9.

49–50 Katherine makes this reply at a point later on in F, when Henry tries to tell her in French that she is the most beautiful lady in the world (TLN 3204–5).

49 de best Q's version of F's 'de most sage'.

50 Q invents Henry's denial, and then reverts to a shorter version of the next exchange in the F sequence, where Katherine's reply also belongs.

53–61 Q paraphrases Henry's next speech in F, where the Constantinople reference (lines 29–30) comes from. The gist of this speech comes from earlier in F, a passage omitted by Q from Henry's first long speech, lines 23–30.

62 the . . . father In F Katherine says '*de Roy mon pére.*' Henry's reply follows in Q as in F, but with Katherine's response cut.

64 kiss you Q's version of F's 'kisse your Hand, and I call you my Queene.' In fact Henry aims for the mouth.

65–6 Katherine's French in Q here bears no relation to her French in F. For the French '*baiser*', which is heavily played on in both versions, Q offers '*quelque chose*'. Q's last word of her protest, 'fouor', does not have any easy relation phonetically to a comprehensible word in French. The French '*faveur*' here is conjectural, based on Q2's change, so that Q makes Katherine say 'this fashion of yours is not at all in favour'. Alice offers a roughly equivalent gloss for such a statement. Q omits Henry's offer to kiss her lips instead, and Katherine's elaboration in French about

it not being the custom to kiss before marriage, which for all the omission the Q
Henry takes up in line 70.

72 *Oui . . . grace* F has the less polite but more accurate '*Ouy verayment*', phonetic for
'Oui, vraiment'.

73–6 The last speech in the wooing scene is again much shorter in Q than in F, but it
keeps the reference to her witchcraft being most persuasive. The last sentence,
invariably comic in all stagings, as the hurried line in F, 'Heere comes your father',
indicates, in Q is the neutral 'Your father is returned'. His greeting to them is
peculiar to Q.

78–9 Q cuts almost seventy lines of badinage from the courtiers to Henry, especially
from Burgundy, but also from the French king, and comes straight to the political
point. The French king's answer to Henry's demand is invented by Q, along with
Exeter's immediate explanation. In F he merely says 'Wee haue consented to all
tearmes of reason', and Westmorland expands, saying that he has agreed to Henry
marrying Katherine, and all the other Articles with one exception, which Exeter
names.

80–9 Exeter's lines are almost exactly the same in Q and F.

87 *Et* **heir** *de* The one difference in Exeter's French from the F version is the
anglicisation of F's '*heritier de France*'. It may well have been felt necessary to
emphasise this crucial word with an English expression, since it gives the political
explanation why it was necessary for Henry to marry Katherine, ramified by the
denial of Salic Law in the opening scene.

95–6 This couplet in Q paraphrases eight lines by the French king in F.

97–102 Q retains Henry's final rhyming couplet, but cuts Henry's comment to Burgundy in F about 'suretie of our Leagues'.

102 F calls for a '*Senet*' or celebratory trumpet-call before the general '*Exeunt*'. Q has
no such note, nor even an exit direction.

APPENDIX 1

Some of Q's re-lining of verse

1.172–4   This he returnes.
        He saith,theres nought in *France* that can be with a nimble
        Galliard wonne : you cannot reuel into Dukedomes there:

1.186–9   That all the Courts of *France* shall be disturbd with chases.
        And we understand him well,how he comes ore vs
        With our wilder dayes,not measuring what use we made
                      of them.

1.218–20   Therefore let our collectiõ for the wars be soone prouided:
        For God before,weell check the Dolphin at his fathers
                                 (doore.

3.37–42   If litle faults proceeding on distemper should not bee
                          (winked at,
        How should we stretch our eye,when capitall crimes,
        Chewed,swallowed and disgested,appeare before vs:
        Well yet enlarge the man,tho Cambridge and the rest
        In their deare loues,and tender preseruation of our state,

3.97–102 Whose ruine you haue sought,
        That to our lawes we do deliuer you.   (death,
        Get ye therefore hence:poore miserable creatures to your
        The taste whereof,God in his mercy giue you   (amisse:
        Patience to endure,and true repentance of all your deeds
        Beare them hence.

5.72–6   *Dol.* Say that my father render faire reply,
        It is against my will:
        For I desire nothing so much,
        As oddes with England.
        And for that cause according to his youth
        I did present him with those *Paris* balles.

6.25–7   Or like to men proud of destruction,defie vs to our worst,
        For as I am a souldier,a name that in my thoughts
        Becomes me best,if we begin the battery once againe

9.107–10 Did march three Frenchmens.
        Yet forgiue me God,that I do brag thus:

This your heire of *France* hath blowne this vice in me.
I must repent,go tell thy maister here I am,

II.93–5   May not appall their courage.
O not to day,not to day ô God,
Thinke on the fault my father made,
In compassing the crowne.

APPENDIX 2

Q's rendering of Pistol's lines as verse

2.21–2   Base slave,callest thou me hoste?
Now by gaddes lugges I sweare,I scorne the title,
Nor shall my *Nell* keepe lodging.

2.31–4   Solus egregious dog,that solus in thy throte,
And in thy lungs,and whichis worse,within
Thy messfull mouth,I do retort that solus in thy
Bowels, and in thy Iaw,perdie: for I can talke,
And *Pistolls* flashing firy cock is vp.

2.39–40   O braggard vile,and damned furious wight,
The Graue doth gape,and groaning
Death is neare,therefore exall.

2.46–50   Couple gorge is the word,I thee defie agen :
A damned hound,thinkst thou my spouse to get?
No,to the powdering tub of infamy,
Fetch forth the lazar kite of Cresides kinde,
Doll Tear-sheete,she by name, and her espowse
I haue,and I will hold,the quandom quickly,
For the onely she and Paco,there it is inough.

2.65–8   A noble shalt thou haue,and readie pay,
And liquor likewise will I giue to thee,
And friendship shall combind and brotherhood :
Ile liue by *Nim* as *Nim* shall liue by me :
Is not this iust ? for I shall Sutler be
Vnto the Campe,and profit will occrue.

6.2–3   Tis hot indeed,blowes go and come,
Gods vassals drop and die.

6.6–7   And I. If wishes would prevaile,
I would not stay,but thither would I hie.

9.19–21   *Bardolfe* a souldier, one of buxsome valour,
Hath by furious fate
And giddy Fortunes fickle wheele,
That Godes blinde that stands vpon the rowling restlesse
(stone.

9.29–35   Fortune is *Bardolfes* foe,and frownes on him,
     For he hath stolne a packs,and hanged must he be:
     A damned death,let gallowes gape for dogs,
     Let man go free,and let not death his windpipe stop.
     But *Exeter* hath giuen the doome of death,
     For packs of pettie price :
     Therefore go speake the Duke will heare thy voyce,
     And let not *Bardolfes* vitall threed be cut,
     With edge of penny cord,and vile approach.
     Speake Captaine for his life,and I will thee requite.

11.10–12 A lad of life,an impe of fame :
     Of parents good,of fist most valiant:
     I kiss his durtie shoe:and from my hart strings
     I loue the louely bully.What is thy name?

18.10–11 Ha,art thou bedlem?
     Dost thou thurst base Troyan,
     To haue me fold vp *Parcas* fatall web?
     Hence,*I* am qualmish at the smell of Leeke.

BIBLIOGRAPHY

Henry V: Parallel Texts of the First Quarto (1600) and First Folio (1623) Editions, ed. B. R. Nicholson, with an introduction by P. A. Daniel, London: W. Griggs, 1887.

Berger, Thomas L. 'The Printing of *Henry V*, Q1', *The Library*, 6th series, 1 (1979), 114–25.

Blayney, Peter W. M. '"Compositor B" and the Pavier Quartos: Problems of Identification and their Implications', *The Library* 27 (1972), 179–206.

Brown, Ivor. *Shakespeare and the Actors*, London: Bodley Head, 1970.

Cairncross, Andrew S. 'Quarto Copy for Folio *Henry V*', *Studies in Bibliography* 8 (1956), 67–93.

Crane, David. *The Merry Wives of Windsor*, Cambridge: Cambridge University Press, 1997.

Davison, Peter. (ed.) *The First Quarto of King Richard III*, Cambridge: Cambridge University Press, 1996.

Duthie, G. I. 'The Quarto of Shakespeare's *Henry V*', in *Papers, Mainly Shakespearian*, Edinburgh: Oliver & Boyd, 1964, pp. 106–30.

Halio, Jay L. (ed.) *The First Quarto of King Lear*, Cambridge: Cambridge University Press, 1994.

Hart, Alfred. *Stolne and Surreptitious Copies: A Comparative Study of Shakespeare's Bad Quartos*, Melbourne: Melbourne University Press, 1942.

Ioppolo, Grace. *Revising Shakespeare*, Cambridge, Mass.: Harvard University Press, 1991.

Irace, Kathleen. 'Reconstruction and Adaptation in Q *Henry V*', *Studies in Bibliography* 44 (1991), 228–53.

Reforming the 'Bad' Quartos: Performance and Provenance of Six Shakespearean First Editions, Newark, NJ: University of Delaware Press, 1994.

Irace, Kathleen. (ed.) *The First Quarto of Hamlet*, Cambridge: Cambridge University Press, 1998.

Loehlin, James N. *Shakespeare in Performance: 'Henry V'*, Manchester: Manchester University Press, 1996.

McMillin, Scott. 'Casting the *Hamlet* Quartoes: The Limit of Eleven', in *The 'Hamlet' First Published (Q1, 1603): Origins, Form, Intertextualities*, ed. Thomas Clayton, Newark, NJ: University of Delaware Press, 1992, pp. 179–94.

Maguire, Laurie E. *Shakespearean Suspect Texts: The 'Bad' Quartos and Their Contexts*, Cambridge: Cambridge University Press, 1996.

Simison, Barbara Damon. 'A Source for the First Quarto of *Henry V*', *MLN* 46 (1931), 514–15.

Smith, Robert A. H. 'Thomas Creede, *Henry V* Q1, and *The Famous Victories of Henrie the Fifth*', *Review of English Studies* 49 (1998), 60–4.

Taylor, Gary. 'Shakespeare's Leno: *Henry V* IV.v.14', *NQ* 224 (1979), 117–18.

Teague, Frances. *Shakespeare's Speaking Properties*, Toronto: Bucknell University Press, 1991.

Walker, Alice. 'Some Editorial Principles (with special reference to *Henry V*)', *Studies in Bibliography* 8 (1956), 95–111.

Walter, J. H. (ed.) *Henry V*, London: Methuen (New Arden Shakespeare), second edn, 1960.

Wells, Stanley, and Taylor, Gary. *Modernising Shakespeare's Spelling, with Three Studies in the Text of 'Henry V'*, Oxford: Clarendon Press, 1979.

Wright, George T. *Shakespeare's Metrical Art*, Berkeley: University of California Press, 1988.

Printed in the United Kingdom
by Lightning Source UK Ltd.
127590UK00002B/105/A